WOMEN PAY THE PRICE

WOMEN PAY THE PRICE
STRUCTURAL ADJUSTMENT
IN AFRICA AND THE CARIBBEAN

EDITED BY
GLORIA THOMAS-EMEAGWALI

Africa World Press, Inc.

P.O. Box 1892
Trenton, New Jersey 08607

Africa World Press, Inc.

P.O. Box 1892
Trenton, NJ 08607

Copyright © 1995 Gloria Thomas-Emeagwali

First Printing 1995

Book Design: Jonathan Gullery
Cover Design: Linda Nickens

Library of Congress Cataloging-in-Publication Data

Women pay the price : structural adjustment in Africa and the
    Caribbean / edited by Gloria Thomas-Emeagwali.
        p.   cm.
    Includes bibliographical references and index.
        ISBN 0-86543-428-X. - - ISBN 0-86543-429-8 (pbk.)
        1. Structural adjustment (Economic policy) - - Developing countries -
- Case studies. 2. Poor women - -Developing countries- -Case studies.
3. World Bank- -Developing countries- -Case studies. 4. International
Monetary Fund - -Developing countries - -Case studies. I. Thomas
-Emeagwali, Gloria, 1950–
HC59.7.W636   1994
338.9.' 0082- -dc20
                                                    94-40497
                                                        CIP

CONTENTS

Dedication...vii

Acknowledgement..ix

Preface...xi

1.   Introductory Perspectives: Monetarists, ...1
      Liberals and Radicals: Contrasting Perspectives
      on Gender and Structural Adjustment
      Gloria Thomas-Emeagwali

2.   Structural Adjustment and 13
      Gender in Guinea Bissau
      Rosemary Galli and Ursula Funk

3.   The Impact of Structural Adjustment 31
      on Maternal and Child Health in Nigeria
      Folasode Iyun

4.   Structural Adjustment and Female Wage Labor 39
      in the Nigerian Textile Industry
      Adebayo and Hussainatu Olukoshi

5.   Crisis and Structural Adjustment in 53
      Sierra Leone: Implications for Women
      A. Zack-Williams

6.   Gender and Adjustment: Pictures from Ghana...........63
      Lynne Brydon and Karen Legge

7.   Engendering the Adjustment Process............................87
     in Trinidad and Tobago: Perspectives
     and Policy Issues
     Gwendoline Williams and Ralph Henry

8.   Guyanese Women in Action: 105
     Response and Reactions to Economic Reform
     Adeline Apena

9.   Possibilities for Cushioning the Adverse Effects 121
     of the Structural Adjustment Programs
     on Vulnerable Women in Zambia
     Mosebjane Malatsi

10. Economic Crisis, Structural Adjustment 133
     and Africa's Future
     Julius Ihonvbere

     Profiles of Contributors 155

     Index 159

To Winnie Mandela
who kept the fire burning and never gave up though
hounded and persecuted by the agents and agencies
of white supremacy.

ACKNOWLEDGEMENT

Special thanks go to Mary and Ben Turok for support and assistance rendered in the publication of this text in its early stage.

PREFACE

The various programs of economic reform associated with the newly independent states of the former Soviet Union and Eastern Europe bring into focus reform processes being implemented elsewhere. In this text we look at parts of Africa and the Caribbean with specific attention to the differential effects of various structural adjustment reform programs within sectors and between one sector and another. The progressive feminization of poverty seems to be a general trend in the regions of focus and one of the objectives of this text is to subject this issue to scholarly research and academic scrutiny. The programs have been seen by some scholars as instrumental in the recolonization of former colonies by the West. Others have associated them with IMF/World Bank imperialism. Indirectly and otherwise we address these issues.

This text was initially conceived in 1990 during my sabbatical year at St. Anthony's College, Oxford University. The weekly seminars at Queen Elizabeth House, also at Oxford, proved quite useful given the intellectual discourse which they stimulated on the issue of gender relations and cross-cultural gender research. Equally significant was the Institute for African Alternatives, London, which proved a useful avenue for the exploration of some of the issues discussed in the text, particularly in the embryonic stages of the project. The contributors to the text include senior government consultants, policy analysts, sociologists, economists and historians, all of whom shed light on the multidimensional impact of IMF and World Bank influenced Structural Adjustment Programs, as they affect Africa and the Caribbean.

Gloria T. Emeagwali
African Studies, CCSU, New Britain

CHAPTER ONE

INTRODUCTORY PERSPECTIVES MONETARISTS, LIBERALS AND RADICALS: CONTRASTING PERSPECTIVES ON GENDER AND STRUCTURAL ADJUSTMENT IN AFRICA

Gloria Thomas-Emeagwali

Three schools of thought seem to have emerged over the last decade with respect to the analysis and critique of structural adjustment programs in Africa. Each has specific implications not only for the definition of structural adjustment but also because of their philosophical underpinnings, for sensitivity to gender issues, and their perceptions of the significance of women in the so-called adjustment process. We may classify these schools of thought as (1) the monetarist-cum-neoclassical school, (2) the liberal or neoliberal school, and (3) the radical, which itself encompasses dependency theorists, marxists, neo-marxists and thinkers of the old and new left.

The first group, the monetarist-cum-neoclassical, tends to view the issue largely in microeconomic and macroeconomic terms and the economic crisis preceding the adoption of structural adjustment programs is explained in terms of irrational behavior, inefficiency, and undue state interventionism.[1] The IMF/World Bank prescription is perceived as constituting a body of remedial policies aimed at re-establishing equilibrium by means of stabilization and adjustment phases. The first phase is seen as the reduction of domestic absorption and the second — that is, adjustment — as addressing supply-side policies such as the promotion of the export of primary materials.[2] The analysis employed is usually technical and static and tends to endorse the IMF/World Bank conditionalities, namely, currency devaluation, the deregulation of prices, privatization of parastatals, trade liberalization, and the removal of subsidies on food, petrol, health, and other services.[3] Of course each of these conditionalities has implications for gender analysis.

Initially most analysts utilizing the monetarist/neoclassical framework of analysis tended to claim gender neutrality and to feverishly deny the accusation of being implicitly patriarchal if not by sins of omission, at least by the overall inclination to assume that the price mechanism and the free market economy meant the same thing for both genders. More recently, however, there has been a subtle shift away from this position. It is not inconceivable that Elson's 1987 critique of mainstream economics on the question of gender and structural adjustment played a crucial role in destablishing the earlier position, given the fact that this well-argued piece displayed undeniable familiarity and knowledge of the rules of the neo-classical game and was argued well within the framework of mainstream economics.[4] Appleton's work on the gender dimensions of structural adjustment refers specifically to the role of quantitative analysis and orthodox economic theory and is one of the indicators of compromise on the part of the practitioners of mainstream economics.[5]

Appleton's argument is that by identifying the sectors differentially affected by the various components of the program we can identify those cases where limited intersectoral mobility exists, and focus on cases where women are skewed into particular sectors. He suggests that through the analysis of household data sets, gender differences can be actually quantified. Elson, for her part, had specified in her pioneering work that the disaggregation and separation of the private sector into formal and informal, and foreign owned and locally owned sectors, would lead to a more balanced gender analysis, since such an analysis would highlight the fact that there was a shift of costs from the paid economy to the unpaid economy and that women's labor was in fact being made to compensate for the shortfall. Elson also stressed that the reproduction and maintenance of human resources in the market economy was perpetuated by unequal gender relations and that women generally competed in the market on the basis of unequal terms, given the multiple burdens imposed on them simultaneously. Women were affected by the changes in the level and composition of public expenditure, increases in charges for services, changes in working conditions, and overall changes in income: all associated with structural adjustment programs in various African countries. The fundamental difference between the analyses of Elson and Appleton lies in the degree of faith and optimism manifested by the latter in the market. There are some other important differences and these we hope to highlight in the discussion which follows for, whilst Appleton fits neatly into the first category identified and is indisputably inclined to the monetarist-cum-neoclassical school, Elson perhaps fits more accurately in the second grouping, namely, the liberal school.

Scholars associated with liberal scholarship, while generally utilizing the tools of orthodox economic analysis, tend to deemphasize the significance of the market.[6] Generally they are more receptive to state interventionism and are less enamored of the price mechanism and laissez faire policies. They are less technicist and economistic in argument and more flexible in their definition and interpretation of efficiency, irrationality, risk taking, and other concepts so dear to the orthodox neoclassical position. The slogan "adjustment with a human face" is basically compatible with their view. They are more consistently receptive to engendering their analysis, and more prone to writing women into their economic postulations.[7] They argue more consistently than their colleagues that women are affected by the structural adjustment programs in their various capacities as producers, home managers, mothers and community leaders, and so on, since they serve in these various capacities, often simultaneously.[8]

As producers, women are affected by job cuts and retrenchment in the public sector, where they had gained a foothold in some countries, and, in the agrarian sector, by declining terms of trade. The reallocation of investible funds from the food crop sector to the export and cash crop sectors has also affected them negatively since they seem to have been dominant in the former sphere in most areas. Women play a leading role in the sale of local fast foods and small scale food processing, and are directly affected by the decline in purchasing power of their clientele.[9] As home managers and mothers they are affected by expenditure cuts and the removal of subsidies on food and items such as fuel, etc., and are affected by cuts in health, education, and other social services.[10] This is more so where women head households but is also applicable in other contexts since they are often expected to continue with household management on the lines of the pre-structural adjustment budget.[11] In many cases the old allowances for running the household remain. In others they have shrunk or no longer exist, given the high incidence of retrenchment and unemployed husbands.[12] For women, life after the adoption of a structural adjustment program is even worse than before, because they have to spend more time and energy in search of fewer commodities and less time is left for social activities in the community. Scholars such as Collier and Appleton, Elson, and Callaghy seem to fall within the framework of analysis of the two schools of thought so far cited.[13]

We shall now focus on the third perspective on structural adjustment and gender and examine the basic propositions implied by scholars such as Onimode, Mamdani, Amin, Antrobus, Girvan, and others[14] who point out that the structural adjustment offensive deployed by the twin institutions of the IMF and World Bank is being embarked on primarily in the context of the refusal of western economies to adjust to a slowdown in the global economy and excess capacity. They argue that the programs at best aim at the integration of peasant production into the world commodity market — in the context of global capitalist expansion — and that they are catalysts not for growth and development but for the destruction of embryonic industries and the overall intensification of maldevelopment in these areas. They do not attempt to halt the process of capital transfer and decapitalization, nor do they aim at sustained economic growth in these regions.[15]

Structural adjustment in IMF/World Bank terms is not merely a bout of stabilization followed by adjustment; nor is it simply an innocuous remedial package for sustained growth and development; rather, it is seen by most scholars associated with the radical interpretation as an almost deliberate scheme for the perpetuation of export dependency, maverick and unfavorable interest rates, fluctuating terms of trade, and the reproduction of existing conditions of global inequality.[16] Some of these conditions caused the problem of insolvency and massive indebtedness in the first place and, in their view, it is irrational to propose that such conditions would not worsen and intensify with such a package.[17]

We should point out that the degree of sensitivity to gender issues is not uniform within the radical school of thought. There are several instances where the focus on north/south interaction and the issue of mass poverty as a whole predominates over a more clinical analysis of the intersection of gender and class. Moreover in several instances the focus on class has been at the expense of gender sensitivity. On the whole, however, in the more exemplary accounts, an attempt is made to grapple with the woman question in the context of the phenomenon of structural adjustment.

In general terms there is an overview perception that women, by virtue of their overall centrality in production, including their role in the household and in the economy at large, bear the brunt of the phenomenal system of dislocation associated with the IMF\World Bank package of conditionalities.[18] They have devised methods for coping with the new situation but the discomfort which they are forced to endure should not be underestimated.

In her focus on women, work, and ideology in a context of economic crisis, Pittin has pointed out that in Nigeria the economic crisis has affected women in different ways, thus highlighting the differentiation taking place between specific groups of women.[19] She points out, for example, that elite women now trade in costly goods, using their contacts, position, and available and preexisting wealth to enhance commercial gains. These women use affinal, kinship, and professional networks to expand their trading activities and, unlike their poorer counterparts, they have the encouragement and opportunity to pursue higher education. This is a far cry from the case of the Karuwai (a Hausa term referring to prostitutes) who eke out a precarious livelihood and find themselves unable to mobilize the capital to participate in the distributive sector. They are victimized by local, traditional, state, and federal authorities and are marginalized both ideologically and economically.

Similar gender-sensitive analyses have been made for other parts of Africa, and there is clearly a need for more of these so as to facilitate our understanding of the conditions of existence of women under structural adjustment, in a situation where some are more oppressed than others and the various conditionalities have a differential impact.[20] It seems that the 'liberals' and 'radicals' offer the most relevant methodological tools for accomplishing this objective.

The chapters in this text cover Nigeria, Guinea-Bissau, Ghana, and Sierra Leone in West Africa, and Zambia in Southern Africa. Comparative inferences are drawn with reference to the impact of structural adjustment on the position of women in Trinidad and Tobago and Guyana in the Caribbean region. There is a focus on maternal and child health care, the industrial sector, and various coping mechanisms. Generally the work provides documentation and interpretation of prevailing systems of adjustment and maladjustment in various parts of the African continent. Julius Ihonvbere, in the concluding chapter, emphasizes that, generally speaking, structural adjustment programs have accentuated the delegitimatization of the state, have led to political instability, and have brought about severe economic dislocation. Class contradictions have been intensified and the economic and ecological arenas severely dislocated by higher debt, increased debt-servicing ratios, and inflation, and (with reference to the environment) by the reckless exploitation of natural resources by desperate elites. Ihonvbere thoroughly discusses various reasons why the programs have in fact failed and by doing so contributes to the general discourse on the constraints and obstacles associated with the economic reform process. The overall purpose of this volume is not only to provoke a reassessment of the various existing methodologies but also to generate comments and recommendations for coping analytically and otherwise with the present crisis.

The phenomenon of female-headed households has been identified in most of the chapters of this text. In all cases, such women and their dependents are identified as constituting a major percentage of the vulnerable population, where vulnerability is associated with deprivation and inaccessibility to necessary and basic goods and services required to meet basic physical, psychological, and socioeconomic needs in socially and environmentally sustainable ways. Female heads of households tend to be discriminated against in terms of land ownership, access to hired labor, receipt of inputs such as fertilizers, and other relevant variables.

Such women, be they widows, divorcees, or separated, single mothers, women with husbands absent for prolonged periods, or teenage mothers (categories which are by no means mutually exclusive), tend to have a high incidence of malnutrition in their households. According to Malatsi, they work harder and for longer hours than their male counterparts. Extension staff invariably discriminate against them in their capacity as female farmers. In Nigeria, the demolition of stalls, kiosks, and so-called illegal structures affected those who were petty traders. We may note, however, that the majority of this population came from the agrarian sector and were basically rural. Iyun points out that the anthropometric ratio for Nigerian children was worse in 1988 than in the 1960s. A large percentage of these children came from female-headed households and yet the fundamental cause of this state of affairs was of course not the gender of the household head *per se* but the discriminatory and inequitable system of resource-distribution at the local, national, and global levels, as well as the ongoing process of accumulation which continues to intensify deprivation and dependence.

The formulation of programs to cushion the effects of structural adjustment programs was called for as early as 1983. Other programs have since been deployed, including the SDA Social Action Program in Cameroon; the SDA Project in Ghana, which complements Ghana's Program of Action to Mitigate the Social Cost of Adjustment (PAMSCAD); the Grassroots Development Initiatives Project in Togo; the Alleviation of Poverty and Social Costs of Adjustment Project in Uganda; the Social Dimensions of Adjustment Initiative in Mozambique; the Social Development Action Project in Chad; the Economic Management and Social Action Project in Madagascar; and, finally, SDA Projects in Senegal and Guinea-Bissau.

As pointed out by Awgu-Jones,[21] the objective of the SDAs is to strengthen the capacity of participating governments to protect the poor and vulnerable groups from bearing undue hardship as a result of structural adjustment. It is in the light of this that we appreciate the chapters that have focussed largely on such remedial programs.

Galli and Funk have pointed out that up to 1990 one component of the World Bank SDA program for Guinea-Bissau had not even been attempted and some components were at early stages of implementation. The same can be said of the Zambian case although we do have an in-depth analysis of issues to be taken into consideration in designing and implementing such programs.

Needless to say, in the final analysis such remedial policies may tinker with the prevailing system piecemeal and do not by any means imply a fundamental redress either system-wide or on the local level. They do not even attempt to deal with the structural problems and overall issues that brought about the debt crisis in the first place nor do they account for the failure of the funding agencies to anticipate the traumatic effects of the programs initially. Moreover, there are doubts as to whether the various remedial programs have the capability to achieve their publicly declared objectives.

The Trinidad and Tobago case study as well as that of Guyana provide some useful points of reference and comparison. In the first place, we are reminded that the IMF/World Bank mission is transcontinental, with the Third World as its laboratory. Secondly, we are reminded that the failure of the programs to induce growth in Africa has more to do with the inappropriate and ineffective nature of the programs than with their implementation.

Africa and other parts of the Third World have been afflicted with a series of ill-advised and inappropriate development strategies over the last thirty years (not to mention the colonial era). The structural adjustment program must be seen as another in this series of ill-advised policies. It is evident as well that gender equity has been a missing ingredient in all these various concoctions.

Henry and Williams have recommended the development of flexible educational and training programs, the provision of credit to small-scale enterprises, and gender awareness in physical planning, as well as the replacement or modification of the present policy emphasis on fiscal and monetary dimensions with a more interdisciplinary methodology, suggestions which are by no means irrelevant to the African case whether in terms of Guinea-Bissau, Sierra Leone, or any of the other regions. We may add to these some other recommendations, such as the intensive training in health care and nutrition of women's groups, the proliferation of meaningful self-help schemes, and improvement in food preservation, food storage, and water irrigation, suggestions which have been lucidly articulated in the Zambian case.

It seems that we have now come full circle and are indeed back to some of the modest elementary development aspirations of earlier decades following "flag independence." It has been a circuitous and extremely hazardous route indeed. In the long term, however, some of the basic issues are still left unsolved, among them the question of arbitrary hikes in interest rates and therefore overnight indebtedness on a large scale for fledgling economies; unfavorable terms of trade for primary commodities; the increased marginalization of Africa and other Third World economies in the light of developments in Eastern Europe and the former Soviet Union; the continued role of Africa and other Third World economies as the proverbial "hewers of wood and drawers of water" in the context of the international division of labor; and in the domestic arena the systematic plunder and looting of the national treasury by kleptomaniacs in government and the bureaucracy in the context of the maldistribution of resources. Women are directly affected by the perpetuation of these symptoms of maldevelopment and have a formidable battle to fight as we prepare to move into the 21st century.

NOTES

1. For aspects of this view see Ernest Wilson,"Privatization in Africa: Domestic Origins, Current Status and Future Scenarios," *Issue* 15, no. 2 (1988). See also Eboe Hutchful,"From Revolution to Monetarism: The Economics and Politics of the Adjustment Program in Ghana," in Bonnie Campbell and John Loxley, eds. *Structural Adjustment in Africa,* (New York: Macmillan 1989). Paul Collier argues that "the over-riding errors have been macroeconomic" in "From Critic to Secular God: The World Bank and Africa," *African Affairs* 90, no. 358(1991).
2. See R. Lopez and V. Thomas, "Import Dependency and Structural Adjustment in Sub-Saharan Africa," *The World Bank Economies Review* 4, no. 2 (1990). This perspective is also reflected in L. Demersy and T. Addison, *The Alleviation of Poverty under Structural Adjustment* (Washington.D.C.: World Bank, 1987.)
3. See *Report of the Americas* 111, no. 5 (1990). For a non-monetarist analysis, see M. Obadan and B. Ekuerhare, "The Theoretical Basis of Structural Adjustment Programs in Nigeria," *International Social Science Journal* May 1989.
4. This point is illustrated by Dianne Elson in her pioneering article in B. Onimode, ed., *The IMF, The World Bank and African Debt* (London: Zed Books, 1989).
5 S. Appleton, "Gender Dimensions of Structural Adjustment: The Role of Economic Theory and Quantitative Analysis," *IDS Bulletin* 22, no. 1 (1991).
6. See also *Engendering Adjustment in the 1990's,* Report of a Commonwealth Expert Group on Women and Structural Adjustment (London: Commonwealth Secretariat, 1989).
7. G. Cornia, et al., *Adjustment with a Human Face* (Oxford: Oxford University Press, 1987).
8. See note 6.
9. See G. Thomas-Emeagwali," Islam and Gender: The Nigerian Case," in C. Fawzi El-Solh and J. Mabro, eds., *Muslim's Women's*

Choices (Oxford: Berg, 1994).

10. See N. Aguiar and Thais Corral, *Alternatives: Women's Visions and Movements* (Brazil: Development Alternatives with Women for a New Era, 1991).

11. See Carolyne Dennis, "Constructing a Career under Conditions of Economic Crisis and Structural Adjustment: The Survival Strategies of Nigerian Women," in H. Afshar, ed., *Women, Development and Survival in Third World* (London: Longman, 1991).

12. See Thomas-Emeagwali, "Islam and Gender." (1994).

13. Paul Collier, "SDA Analysis Plans: Gender Specific Issues in the Analysis of Survey Data," Unit for the Study of African Economies, Institute of Economic and Statistics, Oxford University, 1990.

14. See B. Onimode, *The IMF, The World Bank and African Debt: The Social and Political Impact*, (London: Institute for African Alternatives/Zed Press, 1989); P. Antrobus, "Strategies for Change: Design or Programs/Plans," Paper presented at the Commonwealth Regional Meeting on Structural Adjustment, Economic Change and Women, Barbados, May 1990.; and G. Beckford and N. Girvan, eds., *Development in Suspense* (Kingston: Freidrich Ebert Stiftung/ Association of Caribbean Economists, 1989).

15. See D. Budhoo, *Enough is Enough,* (New York: New Horizons Press, 1990); A. Hoogvelt, "Debt and Indebtedness: The Dynamics of Third World Poverty," *Review of African Political Economy (ROAPE)* 47 (1990); and Y. Bangura, *Crisis, Adjustment and Politics in Nigeria* (Uppsala: 1989).

16. M. Mamdani and M. Majoub, *Adjustment and Delinking, The African Experience* (London: Zed, 1990).

17. T. Shaw, "Africa's Conjuncture: From Structural Adjustment to Self-Reliance," *Third World Affairs 1988* (N.Y.: Third World Foundation for Social and Economic Studies, 1988). Shaw points out that there is little evidence that the global economy is expanding sufficiently to absorb Africa's exports of raw material as implied by IMF policies for recovery.

18. See Antrobus in Beckford and Girvan, eds., *Development in Suspense*. For direct reference to Africa, see M. Mbilinyi,"Structural Adjustment, Agribusiness and Rural Women in Tanzania," in H. Berstein et al., *The Food Question,* (London: Earthscan, 1990); and Janet Bujra, "Taxing Development: Why Women Must Pay? Gender and Development Debate in Tanzania," *ROAPE* 47 (1990).

19. R. Pittin, *Women, Work, and Ideology in a Context of Economic Crisis: A Nigerian Case Study,* working papers (The Hague:

Institute of Social Studies, 1989).

20. M. Mbilinyi, "Structural Adjustment, Agribusiness" (1990). Dorothy Muntemba, "The Imapct of IMF/World Bank Programs on Women and Children in Zambia," in Onimode, *IMF, World Bank and African Debt.* See also G. Thomas-Emeagwali and R.O. Lasisi, "Food Crisis and Agro-Based Technology in Nigeria," *ROAPE* 4 (1988).

21. A. Awgu-Jones, "The Impact of Structural Adjustment Programs.." Paper presented at the Development Alternatives with Women regional meeting, Ibadan Nigeria, 1991.

CHAPTER TWO

STRUCTURAL ADJUSTMENT AND GENDER IN GUINEA-BISSAU

Rosemary E. Galli and Ursula Funk

The current economic crisis in Africa affects populations unequally, with women and children among the hardest hit. Meena[1] found in Tanzania that "women are always the shock absorbers of economic crisis and failed development policy." In Guinea-Bissau, the situation is more complicated. This chapter shows that structural adjustment policies, which are meant to resolve the crisis, affect producers differentially.

In Guinea-Bissau, around 80% of the population resides and works in the countryside despite a noteworthy if not accelerating rural exodus, particularly to the capital city of Bissau. This is one of several 'survival strategies' that rural populations have adopted in response to economic crisis. While touching briefly on the dilemma of urban populations as structural adjustment policies attempt to reverse urban-rural terms of trade, the focus of this chapter is mainly on rural populations and on women in particular.

The following sections assess the overall state of the economy through 1990 and the impact first of the economic stabilization policies of the first national development plan and then that of the structural adjustment program. The analysis moves from the macroeconomic to the microeconomic level and survival strategies.

THE GUINEAN ECONOMY

Economists have identified Guinea-Bissau's central economic problem as one of imbalance between production and consumption. This is preeminently a political problem because the major producers in the country are small-holding farmers — in certain sectors and geographical areas, the majority are women — whereas the major consumers are non-productive, service sector urban residents.[2] The greatest consumer of all has been the government. From 1974 when independence was granted through 1983, the government pursued a policy which attempted to make agriculture pay for state investment in relatively large-scale industries that produced next to nothing and certainly nothing for the countryside. As revenues never met expenditures, the government resorted to international borrowing and to expanding the money supply. It also tried to maintain an artificially high exchange rate for the Guinean peso which reinforced unfavorable terms of trade for agriculture. Producers stopped producing, smuggled their production out of the country, or migrated themselves. State marketing agencies monopolized the declining marketing of agricultural crops.

Table 1.
Sales to state marketing agencies, 1978-1981 (tons)[3]

Product	1978	1979	1980	1981
Rice, paddy	1,915	11,824	6,016	1,547
Groundnuts	18,585	18,418	15,683	6,475
Palm oil	156	92	10	12

Source: Galli, 1991a.[4]

Initial government efforts from 1983 to 1986 to reverse this situation brought mixed results. Briefly, policy aimed at increasing production and reducing urban and government consumption through a radical devaluation of the Guinean peso, a substantial increase in farmgate prices, and a cautious liberalization of commerce. At the end of 1983, the peso was initially devalued 100% and allowed to slide downward in value.

Producer prices were raised an overall 80% in 1984; further increases did not keep pace with fall of the peso. Government salaries were increased by only 40% in 1984 and annual increases fell consistently behind the rate of inflation. Government employment, which made up over 80% of all salaried work and was located mainly in urban areas, was frozen. In 1985, 630 employees out of around 19,000 were released.

The most positive results of the policies were in the area of staple food production. Rice is the basic food crop in northern and southern regions and millet, sorghum, and maize are the staples of eastern regions. All peoples, however, prefer rice when available. Tables 2 and 3 show unexpected increases in marketed production in response to rising producer prices when compared with the projected increases forecast in the 1983-86 national plan.

Table 2.
Projected* and actual staple food production,
1983-1986 (in 000s tons).

Product	1983	1984	1985	1986
Rice	93.2*	101.3*	110.6*	121.2
	n.a.	105	115	125
Other	42*	44*	47*	51*
cereals	n.a.	60	65	75

Source: Cabellero, 1987:21[5]

In regard to export production, the results were generally disappointing. The production of groundnuts, the primary export in colonial times and for most of the post-independence era, fell dramatically. Table 3 shows that palm kernel exports also fell short of expectation. Nevertheless, unshelled cashew nuts developed as a promising export.

Table 3.
Projected* and actual export production,
1983-1986 (in 000s tons).

Product	1983	1984	1985	1986
Groundnuts	17.4*	19.4*	21.7*	24.3*
	8.3	8.0	4.2	2.45
Palm kernels	8.0*	8.8*	9.7*	10.6*
	5.2	6.8	2.5	7.5
Cashews	4.0*	4.2*	4.5*	5.0*
	2.0	8.0	6.6	5.9

Source: Cabellero, 1987:20.[6]

To a great extent, the drop in groundnut production can be explained by the collapse of export prices, which in 1981 were $618 per ton and in 1986 were $265 per ton. Palm kernel prices fluctuated wildly. Cashew prices, on the other hand, showed an upward tendency until the mid-1980s. In 1981 they were $618 per ton while in 1986 they were quoted at $816 per ton.[7] Overall, however, export earnings did not grow. At the end of the period, they were still around $14 million, the figure for 1983.

Government expenditures grew rather than diminished. Despite the increase in food production, the government continued to import rice, mainly to feed urban populations. In 1986, 26,900 tons of rice were imported. The total import bill remained essentially what it had been during the entire period, around $65 to $70 million. The foreign debt soared from $140 million in 1981 to approximately $320 million in 1986.

In early 1987, the government signed an agreement with the International Monetary Fund and the World Bank to embark upon a three-year structural adjustment program. In 1989, it entered into a second three-year agreement.[8] This chapter covers the first three years, 1987-1989.

The structural adjustment program (SAP) did not change the direction of macro-economic policy; it aimed at reinforcing and strengthening it. In the sectors where the government had previously hesitated to embark upon reform, the combined forces of the IMF, the World Bank, and most of the "donor" community pushed for more decisive action. This was particularly the case in the areas of government expenditure, fiscal responsibility, employment, and conditions of employment.[9] While continuing to stress both the reduction of public and private consumption and the increase of production, the sponsors of the SAP concentrated most of their efforts on restricting consumption. The peso was devalued even more radically, pressures were put on the government to limit and, where possible, cut its budgets, the Ministry of Finances was exhorted to restrain from expanding the money supply. Likewise the Central Bank was to tighten credit. Around one-third of public employees were supposed to be let go, subsidies eliminated, and personal and other taxes raised. So-called market forces were to take care of production. Trade was to be completely liberalized and producer prices raised and guaranteed.

The results of the first phase of the SAP were mixed. Table 4 presents a sampling of the results, taken from both IMF and government reports.[10]

The picture in 1990 was somewhat more positive. The value of the peso stabilized, at least temporarily. The official dollar exchange rate came close to the black market rate in December 1989 and held steady through the first six months of 1990. The import bill increased but so did export earnings, which were projected to give a more or less 30% rate of coverage in 1990.

In February 1990, a Treasury official announced that government revenues in 1989 had covered government wages and salaries, a rare event in Guinea-Bissau. Government expenditures, however, had also increased — around threefold during the period. The difference between expenditures and revenues was still made up by foreign grants and loans. The foreign debt climbed to around $420 million.

Table 4.
The macroeconomic picture, 1987–1989.

	1987	1988	1989 (projected)
GNP growth (%)	5.6	4	5
Growth of agriculture (%)	10.5	7	6
Growth of real per capita income (%)	1	1	1.5
Inflation rate (%)[11]	99	60	70
Increase in money supply (%)	65	72.8	21
Exchange rate (annual mean pesos per $)	559.83	1100	1800
Differential between official and parallel market rate (%)	170	69	21
Government Revenue excl. grants (billion pesos)	12.58	23.30	39.32
Current expenditures (billion pesos)	15.54	29.47	47.98
Total expenditures (billion pesos)	46.48	88.89	131.20
Govt. revenue incl. grants (billion pesos)	35.21	63.69	121.93
Increase in revenues (%)	194.6	85	69
Revenues/expenditures	72%	79.9%	81.7%
Imports (million US$)	53.6	60.6	62.4
Exports(million $)	15	15.8	18.6
Rate of Coverage	28%	26%	30%
Balance of payments deficit (million $)		14.2	10.5
Debt service (million $)		32.5	34.7
Debt service/exports	136%	92%	130%
Foreign debt (million $)	393	407	420

IMPACT ON THE URBAN POPULATION

The immediate effect of successive and continuing devaluations was a rise in the prices of imported goods, the bulk of which are consumer goods. This hit all sectors of the population but not equally. The rise in basic urban salaries was deliberately designed not to keep pace with the devaluation. By the end of 1988, Lars Rudebeck calculated that the buying power of the urban worker was one-fifth of what it had been in 1983.[12] In a staff report, the World Bank calculated that between 1986 and 1988 there had been a 50% cut in purchasing power. Table 4 shows the official calculation of the overall rate of inflation, but the rate was much higher for the ordinary family. Handem calculated the following rates on normal shopping basket items between 1985 and 1986: cooking oil, 275%; fish, 265%; rice, 66.6%; sugar, 28.5%.[13] An unpublished informal survey by Galli showed that prices in 1989 were significantly higher than in 1987.

Table 5.
Selected prices on the Bissau market.

Product	February 1987	July 1989
Bread	100 PG/kg	200 PG/kg
Sugar	750 PG/kg	2000-5000 PG/kg
Cigarettes	500 PG/pack	2000 PG/pack
Mango	50-100 PG	350 PG/average size
Beer (local)	350 PG/bottle	1000-1300 PG/bottle
Shoes	9000 PG/pair	30,000 PG/pair

As prices rose, families eliminated items from their diets and from their shopping baskets. Meat and fish, for instance, were only eaten in the highest income families.

Rice, however, was the one food that no urban family could do without. Handem calculated that in 1986, 91% of the monthly salary of the lowest government workers was spent on providing rice for the family.[14] The market price she used to reach this calculation was 150 PG per kilo. Moreover, she figured in the government subsidy on a certain ration of rice provided each government worker. In 1989 these subsidies were supposed to have been eliminated and around 5,000 workers fired. In July 1989 there was no rice on the Bissau market. When it could be found, the price had risen to 3000 PG per kilo. By October when the first harvest appeared, the price had fallen to 1200 PG/kg. Calculating the 56 kg needed by the average 8-person family per month to survive at the October price, rice cost the family 66,200 PG or ten times what it had cost in 1986!

Price inflation forced the average government worker, at whatever level, to secure more than one job or income-producing activity. The significance of this was lower productivity in government offices. In the summer of 1989, they emptied at 1:00 P.M. Price inflation meant that almost everyone in the families of urban workers including children had to have some kind of income-generating activity, often falling in the so-called informal or parallel economy. Women abounded in this sector. Having little education, they had little access to salaried employment. The census of 1979 found that only slightly more than 10% of wage workers were women.

During the late 1970s and early 1980s when there was also scarcity, many urban dwellers, especially women, grew their own food in order to cope with food shortages.[15] Around most houses in Bissau and other towns they planted small gardens with vegetables, cassava, and fruit trees. They planted rice during the rainy season in plots on the peripheries of the towns. During the dry season, more enterprising women tried to get access to plots nearby in order to plant irrigated vegetables not only for domestic consumption, but for sale. However, their ability to produce in the urban areas was restricted by the scarcity of unoccupied land.

Another way to make a living for women and men was to take a candonga (bush taxi) to the rural areas in order to buy goods to trade in the urban markets, and to have some food for the "family." Many urban residents still had relatives in the rural areas. When food crises became acute, unemployed women and men went to stay with their rural kin during the rainy season to plant and harvest food for their families.

In 1983 and 1984 large numbers of people went to the South on trucks or ships to procure rice from farmers in this rice-producing region. (In 1989, this strategy was limited because large traders had sent fleets to the South to buy rice. The question on everyone's mind in Bissau that summer was: Where had the rice gone?) The more fortunate urban dwellers were able to rely on kin networks, others had to go to the communities and plead with the farmers to sell them their preferred staple, rice.

Several studies conducted in 1987 showed that urban residents were still resorting to the survival strategies reported by Funk.[16] A study of the informal sector in urban areas showed around 29,000 participants or around 16% of the active population.[17] Another study of one of the neighborhoods of Bissau, Cupelon, in which many of the lowest paid government functionaries live, showed it to be at the heart of the informal economy. This study focused on the women of the neighbourhood, 2,090 of whom were interviewed. It showed these women — most of whose husbands worked for the government — to be active in three areas of activities at the same time: domestic work, agricultural production, mainly market gardening and the marketing of their produce. To supplement the family income and diet, the women had turned themselves into market women. Moreover, during times of agricultural harvesting, they went back to their villages to help in the harvest and, in this way, gained access to rice, palm oil, and other essential items.[18]

Scarcity and economic crisis often increased domestic conflicts and even led to divorce. Marrying more than one wife became problematic for urban men. Women with little economic capacity ran the risk of being abandoned with their children. Thus, women and children often suffered more from the crisis, and gender antagonisms increased because of macro-level processes. There are, unfortunately, no studies on this domestic aspect of the ongoing socioeconomic crisis.

IMPACT ON RURAL POPULATIONS

The price of rice affected rural populations differentially. In the rice surplus-producing South, the spectacular rise in market prices in 1989 affected producer prices in a positive way. Perhaps for the first time in the history of the region and certainly since independence. there was a reversal of the terms of trade in the region's favor. For the first time in fifty years, there was price competition in Tombali which bid producer prices up to between 500 and 1000 PG per kilo, a rise of 150% to 500% over prices in 1988 and 500% to 1000% over 1987.

In regions producing groundnuts, palm kernels, and cashew nuts the dramatic rise in rice prices had a negative impact in

1989. These were generally rice-deficit areas and rice was often exchanged in barter for these export crops.

All areas and all producers were affected by the price rises in basic consumer goods such as cooking oil, tobacco, soap, shoes, matches, and so on, most of which is imported from abroad. Rural producers also had to cope with the prices of capital goods, i.e., tools, whose prices had risen even more steeply than the producer price of rice (see Table 6). Price inflation was not simply the result of successive devaluations but also reflected the speculation of the newly formed merchant class. Trade liberalization caused a redistribution of income toward traders.

Table 6.
Selected prices in farm inputs, 1985-1987.

Product	1985	1987	% Rise
Hoe	325 PG	2500 PG	769%
Plough	6500 PG	132000 PG	2030%
Ox cart	15100 PG	237500 PG	1573%
Donkey cart	14650 PG	233500 PG	1594%
NDK fertilizer	9 PG/kg	220 PG	2444%
Urrea	12 PG/kg	172 PG	1433%

Source: Fonseca, 1989: 11, 12.[19]

Producer prices of major commodities had not kept pace with these rises.

Table 7.
Producer prices, 1985-1987

Product	1985	1987	% Rise
Paddy rice	24 PG/kg	50 PG/kg	208%
Hulled rice	42.5 PG/kg	95 "	224%
Groundnuts	25 PG/kg	40 "	160%
Cashews	28.5 PG/kg	125 "	439%

Source: Fonseca, 1989: 11, 12.[20]

Tables 6 and 7 together show that unfavorable terms of trade continue to plague rural producers despite the SAP. Urban-rural terms of trade had not been reversed. Rudebeck shows how sharply they had deteriorated for the groundnut producers in Kanjadja in northeastern Oio.

Table 8.
Terms of trade for groundnuts on selected items in Kanjadja

Merchandise	1976	1988
Cigarettes (pack)	2.1 kg (groundnuts)	4.5 kg (groundnuts)
1 kg. rice	2.7 "	6.8 "
1 litre cooking oil	6.2 "	24.1 "
1 bicycle	889.0 "	2273.0 "

Source: Rudebeck, 1989: 37[21]

RURAL SURVIVAL STRATEGIES

It has already been noted that outmigration to urban areas is a survival strategy for rural peoples in the face of economic crisis. The World Bank estimated an annual urban growth rate of 6%. This involved men more than women, particularly young unmarried males. Another strategy they used was seasonal migration to Senegal to harvest groundnuts. Some women migrated to Bissau, Zinguinchor, Dakar and even Portugal to perform domestic and other services. Most women, however, remained in rural areas. There were whole areas where villages consisted mainly of women, young children, and the elderly. Like their urban counterparts, rural women in a number of areas of Guinea-Bissau have opted for a role in marketing agricultural produce in order to improve their income. In addition, they also engaged in cooperative activities.

Women's associations have been promoted by rural development projects in northern, eastern, and southern regions of the country and, on a reduced scale, by the National Union of Democratic Women (UDEMU). Northern women band together because the temporary emigration of men in such regions as Cacheu has essentially feminized the rural economy. Women are left to cultivate on their own with the help of young boys.

They band together in village associations for a number of purposes, for example, buying factors of production to lighten their work loads and planting communal seed crops or even a common cereals plot for needy families. In one village, a soap-manufacturing venture was launched; in another, women began by growing tomatoes for markets. This enterprise so expanded that they were able to hire men to process and package the tomatoes for commercial use in hotels and institutions.

In the East, the American Friends Service Committee sponsored a vegetable-growing enterprise which supplied both Bafata and Bissau markets. The women gardened individually but pooled their resources to buy a truck for transport and commercialization. There were plans to establish a joint savings and loan fund.

In Tombali in the South women also predominated in the workforce but here there is both emigration and immigration to the region. Women were nearly 53% of the active population in the region as a whole. The main productive activity, as previously noted, is rice-growing in which women have a much greater role than men. Tombali is considered the rice bowl of Guinea-Bissau but groundnuts are also produced and women do most of that work too. They also engage in fishing, in fruit and vegetable growing, and in processing palm oil for marketing as well as consumption. Besides these, women have the normal domestic activities. Yet, despite this heavy work load, in none of the ethnic groups living in this region do women control access to land.

Handem recorded an 18- to 19-hour work day for women in the South.[22] (In an earlier survey in 1984, Ki-Zerbo and Galli recorded similar workloads for women in the East.) In order to lighten their load, women banded together in associations to buy rice-husking machinery, which significantly reduced domestic work by several hours per day; they also acquired palm-pressing machinery. These joint actions have given them more time for market gardening and, as in the East, they bought trucks to help bring produce to market. Moreover, they, too, started a joint savings fund.

OIO

The afore-mentioned survival strategies were extremely precarious because of division of labor along gender lines that had accompanied the commoditization of agriculture during colonial times. In most Guinean societies, males specialized in the production of cash crops for export. This meant that women bore the primary responsibility for food production. Only among the Balanta Brassa — 30% of the country's population — was the production of food a more or less shared task between the sexes.

One aspect of the ongoing economic crisis experienced in both urban areas and the countryside has been the scarcity of cereals brought on by colonial policies, inefficiencies and corruption in the marketing systems, and by cyclical periods of drought, especially in the 1970s and early 1980s. More recently, a lack of rice supplies in certain areas resulted partly from the activities of merchants to enhance profits which included the hoarding of supplies in Bissau.

Scarcity has plagued some areas of the country more than others. In the rice-producing South, food supplies were generally sufficient and surpluses normally existed to export to other areas. However, there was fear in 1989 that the high producer prices would induce farmers to sell even their seed crops. In the summer of that year, rice surpluses were not generally available in Bissau or elsewhere. There was suspicion that traders were selling the rice in neighboring territories for hard currency.

When scarcity of rice or other cereals occurs, women are forced to increase significantly their work loads — much more than men — and to reduce their income-generating activities such as market gardening and commercialization in order to concentrate on fishing and gathering other food sources. However, Balanta Brassa women lost significantly less income than women from other groups. This was directly related to the fact that Brassa men were also absorbed in rice production.

The comparison of Bejaa and Brassa communities in Oio shows how differently they experienced food scarcity.[23] Among the Brassa, the financial loss was more equally divided. Brassa men took a loss in income because during food scarcity they did not sell rice, their major crop for both consumption and sales. They only sold what was necessary to pay taxes.

Brassa women, who are expected to procure the ingredients for the mafe (sauce/stew) that is served on rice or millet, had to spend more time fishing and collecting these supplements, and thus had less time to earn money. However, their loss was less dramatic than for Bejáa women because Brassa women had more income sources.

In the Bejáa community, women bear a greater financial loss than men during times of food scarcity. As the recognized producers and owners of rice, they do not sell any during periods of food shortage because they would be accused of neglecting their children. Consequently, during periods of scarcity women earn significantly less from rice and yams, significant because of the few sources of income they have. Bejáa men reduced their sales of millet, and thus also took a loss, but they also had groundnuts and palm wine as additional sources of income.

Men and women in both communities experience an increasing loss in income when a crisis deepens, but the impact on their financial assets varied culturally. During this phase of a crisis, losses relate not only to gender-based divisions of labor but also to pre-existing gender-based inequalities in income. Bejáa men who produce groundnuts and sell other goods are less vulnerable than Bejáa women. In contrast, Brassa men and Brassa women take comparable cuts in income.

Loss of wealth such as livestock affects individuals differently depending on the size of their herds. Older individuals usually have more animals. Brassa men have the most livestock, and if food shortages last a long time they are severely affected. Bejáa men and women might take comparable losses depending on the number of animals they own. Thus, among the Brassa the exchange of livestock for food which has to be shared with kin can decrease economic inequalities by gender. In contrast, among the Bejáa such exchange may increase gender inequalities by further weakening women's economic base.

THE CONSEQUENCES FOR WOMEN

The most serious consequence of the female work load at the

level of the individual is poor health. A recent UNICEF study found that 74% of all women have iron-deficiency anemia. This is linked with a high incidence of parasites. Sixty percent of all women carry hepatitis B antibodies while 10% of the population tested seropositive for the AIDS virus. Forty-five percent of Bissau women have sexually transmitted diseases. Hospital records show a high rate of maternal mortality — 6% for Bissau and perhaps as much as 10% in the countryside. This was very high in comparison with such other "Third World" countries as Cape Verde (where the rate was 1.07%), Senegal (with 0.6%), Egypt (with 0.93%), and El Salvador (with 0.69%).

The poor state of women's health has been linked with malnutrition. Even though women are the basic providers, they are the last to eat in the household. Children's health is also at stake: low birthweights are directly tied to female nutrition. Between one in every five to ten children are born at low birthweight. The infant mortality rate — 176 in every 1,000 births — is one of the highest in the world. Around 35% of children under five years of age are said to be suffering from malnutrition.

Recent projects sponsored by the World Bank to relieve the distress and social dislocation caused by the SAP identified women and children as the most vulnerable populations but did very little for them. One component, a national nutrition survey, which might be helpful in planning future projects, had yet to be implemented in 1990. The Social and Infrastructure Relief Project included a job creation scheme which focused on public works across the country, an urban improvement scheme in a middle-class section of Bissau, and retraining and job placement for laid-off government workers, most of which are men.

CONCLUSION

Neither the stabilization policy begun in 1986 nor the first phase of the structural adjustment program can be said to have reversed unfavorable urban-rural or international terms of trade. While the collapse in world market prices for groundnuts complicated matters, it was not at the heart of the macroeconomic problem in Guinea-Bissau as cashew exports compensated for the loss of groundnut earnings. The fundamental problem was social in nature and had to do with the structure of Guinean society promoted by colonial policies. Rural areas—with women carrying the heaviest burden — were expected to pay for urban consumption, the major portion of which has been government expenditure in non-productive activities and investment.

Since 1987, the extraordinary earnings of a merchant class have been added to the rural producers' burden. While the rise in producer prices (and sufficient rainfall) stimulated a substantial increase in both cashew nut collection and food production, thanks largely to the efforts of women, prices have, generally, not kept pace with the falling value of the Guinean peso, rampant inflation, and price speculation. Most producers have suffered a substantial deterioration in their buying power. The spectacular rise in the price of rice in 1989 at least temporarily reversed the terms of trade for those producing enough rice to be able to sell to the market. These were mainly the rice producers in the South. It worked, however, to the disadvantage of the producers of export crops and the women in these groups who bore primary responsibility for production of grains for domestic consumption. There was cultural pressure on them to intensify cereals production, fishing, and gathering of food from other sources to the detriment of income-earning activities.

Forcing women to expand subsistence activities undercuts the possibility of women to improve their economic position, a key factor of which is the availability of discretionary/disposable income both for spending and accumulation. It also strikes at the heart of an agricultural-led development process. The situation could improve if women had direct access to credit for high-yielding production technologies. Rural development projects which have as their objective the attainment of food security have generally paid insufficient attention to women as the major providers of food. The integrated rural development program which covered the northern regions of Cacheu and, to a lesser extent, Oio has not made much headway in helping women raise their productivity in cereals production even though it offered assistance and credit to associations to buy small-scale labor-saving equipment.[24]. The Caboxanque project in Tombali has been much more successful in this regard.

The designers of the Geba Valley rice production project which was located in the eastern regions had not even recognized the sensitive role of women in cereals production and had increased the work load of women without improving their income.[25] There were many other problems with the project, which was abandoned by its donors. The pilot project for women rice growers in the same area funded by the European Union seems to be aware of the need to learn from the mistakes of the previous project.

Although recent development planners have designed projects which contain special programs for women, such as training female extension agents, they continue to downplay women's role as economic actors. Planners tend to allocate benefits such as irrigated perimeters, technology, training, and credit to men who are presumed to be the heads of households. The special programs for women cited above have often been geared to their domestic roles, or supplementary productive activities. Most important of all, the government, despite its stated commitment to the promotion of the equality of women, has not questioned the prevailing gender-based divisions of labor in which women in all ethnic groups in both rural and urban areas work more hours per day than men.

NOTES

1. Meena Ruth, "Crisis and Structural Adjustment: Tanzanian Women's Politics," *Issue* 17, no. 2 (1989).
2. R.E. Galli, "Liberalization is Not Enough: Structural Adjustment and Peasants in Guinea-Bissau," *Review of African Political Economy*, no. 49/50, 1991.
3. One must always exercise a great deal of caution in dealing with statistics on Guinea-Bissau, as the facilities for gathering statistics are still very rudimentary. The authors have generally used official and semi-official statistics as these are cited as the basis for policy-making.
4. Galli, "Liberalization."
5. L. Cabellero, *The Guinea-Bissau: A Study of the Food and Agricultural Sector.* Uppsala: Swedish University of Agricultural Sciences, (1987).
6. *Ibid.*
7. Kelvingate International, Ltd., "Assistence a le reforme du commerce en Guinee-Bissau." March 1987.
8. International Monetary Fund, *Guinea-Bissau: Staff Report on the Request for a Second Annual Arrangement under the Structural*

Adjustment Facility (Washington, D.C., International Monetary Fund, 1989).

9. *Ibid.* See also Galli, "Liberalization," for specifics.
10. International Monetary Fund, *Guinea-Bissau: Staff Report*, and Republica da Guine-Bissau, Ministerio do Plano, *Plano Anual, 1989.* (Bissau: Guine-Bissau, 1989).
11. The IMF figures are 107%, 66% and 40% (projected) respectively.
12. Lars Rudebeck, "Structural Adjustment in a West African Village" in K. Hermele and L. Rudebeck, *At the Crossroads: Political Alliances and Structural Adjustment.* (Uppsala, AKUT, 1989), p. 26.
13. Diana L. Handem, "A Guine-Bissau: o No do Ajustamento," *BISE*, 4, no. 2 (1988). 53–76.
14. *Ibid.*
15. Funk, Ursula, "Labor, Economic Power and Gender," in S.S. Rayna, et al., *The Political Economy of the African Famine* (New York, Gordon and Breach, 1990).
16. *Ibid.*
17. Handem, *"A Guinea-Bissau,"* p. 72.
18. Ana Maria, Delgado, "Relatorio sobre o sector urbano: as Mulheres no sector informal," (Bissau: Instituto Nacional de Estudos e Pesquisas, 1989).
19. J. F. Fonseca, "As Exigencias do Desenvolvimento Rural," *BISE* 5, no. 1 (1989) 1–22.
20. *Ibid.*
21. Rudebeck, "Structural Adjustment in a West African Village."
22. Diana L. Handem, "Relatorio sobre o sector rural: as Mulheres de Cubucare" (Bissau: Instituto Nacional de Estudos e Pesquisas, 1989).
23. Funk, "Labor, Ecomonic Power and Gender."
24. For more information, see R. E., Galli, and J. Jones, *Guinea-Bissau: Politics, Economics and Society* (London and New York, Pinter Publishers and Columbia University Press, 1987).
25. Ibid. Also see A. M. Hochet, *Paysanneries en Atteinte: Guinee-Bissau.* (Dakar: ENDA, 1983).

CHAPTER THREE

THE IMPACT OF STRUCTURAL ADJUSTMENT ON MATERNAL AND CHILD HEALTH IN NIGERIA

Folasade Iyun

Since the late 1980s, many Third World economies have embarked on structural adjustment programs (SAPs) aimed at restructuring the productive base of economies and reducing dependence on the external sector.

A feature of SAPs is the reduction of government expenditure, particularly on social welfare programs. The effect of this is felt especially by vulnerable groups. Mothers and children in particular become marginalized with demonstrable effects on their health and nutritional status.

The effect of structural adjustment on this segment of the Nigerian populace in the next few years can only be imagined, since there seems to be no immediate solution ahead.

This preview attempts to show how a SAP has affected maternal and child health services in Nigeria. Unfortunately, hard data is not easily available. Therefore I have made use of budgetary allocations and clinic hospital attendance figures to measure the impact of the SAP on the health of mothers and young children. Inferences will have to be drawn from this data.

THE IMPACT OF SAP ON EXPENDITURE IN THE HEALTH SECTOR

In 1979, even though Nigeria was already about US $62 million in debt, it still had substantial foreign reserves to enhance its credit worthiness. However, by 1982, the debt problem had exploded with the cost of debt-servicing growing rapidly with the rise in world interest rates. The debt crisis was compounded by the fact that Nigeria had become a principal importer of basic foods such as rice, wheat, and vegetable oils, while her exports of primary products had fallen.

Retrenchment was rampant by 1985 in every state of the Federation that was following the recommendations of organizations like the World Bank and the International Monetary Fund (IMF). The debt crisis was also having a significant impact on health. Budgetary allocations to health had been below 10% in most states since 1982 and there were glaring examples of suspended health projects and abandoned construction sites for health centers and hospitals.

The structural adjustment program introduced in the second half of 1986 was meant to give a new direction to the Nigerian economy, but large-scale retrenchment in government and industry continued, with dire consequences for families with only one breadwinner.

More often than not, budgetary allocations serve merely as political pronouncements, and only a small percentage of the sum allocated is actually spent on health. Yet even available figures point to the downward trend in government expenditure on health: from 4.8% of recurrent expenditure in 1978 to 2.2% in 1989, and from 54% of capital expenditure in 1981 to 1.5% in 1989. This was despite a government commitment to implement Primary Health Care (PHC) at the Federal level.[1]

An examination of recurrent expenditure on health in six

states suggests that these governments cannot afford to drastically reduce this. The trouble is that personal emoluments often take the lion's share of recurrent expenditure, 78% in many states, over 70% at the University Teaching Hospital.[2] and 70%–98% at the local level.[3]

Recently, the prices of basic items such as drugs, dressings, and medical equipment have increased tremendously because of the heavy import component, in a situation in which the local currency (the *naira*) has depreciated almost daily. Increases in budgetary allocations are therefore not reflected in the actual value of services to individuals. We are now in a position in which patients are not only required to purchase all their drugs but to shop for dressings and other medications required for even minor operations. We have thus reached the anomalous situation in which blood transfusions are not possible due to lack of blood-bags for willing donors.

THE IMPACT OF SAP
ON MANPOWER RESOURCES

The number of registered medical practitioners in Nigeria increased six-fold between 1960 and 1979 and a ratio of 1:12,500 had been reached, approaching the World Health Organization target for developing nations. Today, Nigeria cannot retain or maintain her manpower resources either within the public service or the country as a whole. Nigeria is experiencing a disturbing brain drain to the United States, Canada, Western Europe, and the Middle East, especially Saudi Arabia. Reliable data is hard to come by. For instance, reports in the popular press indicate a loss of more than 260 medical specialists in the past three years.

A cursory look at the effect of the brain drain at that renowned center of excellence, the University College Hospital, Ibadan, illustrates the tragedy. Since 1983, 201 medical teaching personnel have resigned or gone on study leave. Over 75% quit in the last four years. A similar trend can be observed for contract and paramedical staff at the hospital.

This downward trend in available skilled manpower can also be seen in many states of the Federation. Since 1982, Ondo State has lost 30% of its medical staff and over 50% of its pharmacists. Some local government areas (LGAs) lost up to 100% between 1982 and 1985, especially to the private sector.[4]

This brain drain has appalling effects on the quality of care available in the affected institutions. Many Nigerians now have little confidence in public medical institutions. A recent study[5] in one LGA in Amambra State showed that only 20.6% of respondents preferred government medical institutions.

THE EFFECTS OF SAP ON MATERNAL AND CHILD HEALTH

A significant effect of the brain drain of medical personnel is the decline in clinic attendance. Indeed, attendance at most medical institutions has declined, not because Nigerians can be said to be getting healthier but due to shortages of basic health care resources and increasing hospital bills.

The downward trend in patient attendance in Niger State is evident from both inpatient and outpatient figures. In 1986, the attendance was less than half that recorded in 1982.[6] Indeed, a decline in clinic/hospital attendance has been the general trend in many parts of Nigeria since the introduction of SAP. For instance, clinic attendance at the International Institute of Tropical Agriculture (IITA) declined by 18% between 1985 and 1988 *despite* free medical care.[7] The decline since 1987 can be explained by the retrenchment of 188 casual workers with about 1,000 dependents who had enjoyed free health care at the clinic.

Attendance at the University College Hospital (UCH), Ibadan, depicts this trend even more vividly. A comparison of attendance in 1982 and in 1986 shows a drastic decline of 48% in outpatient clinic attendance by children.[8] There is a similar trend in the admission of children and women to UCH which cannot be explained by improvement in the health of Nigerian children and their mothers. Thirty-four percent fewer women were admitted to UCH in 1988 than in 1978 and there was a staggering 60% fall in obstetrics admissions. Fewer women now patronize clinics, particularly obstetrics clinics. On the other hand, there appears to be a gradual increase in the number of women attending gynecological clinics, which may imply an increased incidence of diseases associated with female reproduction or we may be tempted to believe that more women in Ibadan are accepting contraception.[9] As regards treatment for nutritional diseases at UCH, the percentage of women receiving treatment dropped from 50% in 1983 to 39% in 1988. During the same period the infant mortality rate remained constant at 120 per 1,000 live births.[10]

Like other hospitals, the UCH, Ibadan, has not had any substantial increase in Federal Government subvention in spite of huge increases in the prices of health resources. As the former Chief Medical Director of the hospital testified, many women can no longer afford the high cost of confinement and delivery, which has increased eight-fold in the last few years.[11] Many women now take the perilous option of delivering at home or at churches.

The SAP package continues to jeopardize the survival chances of women and their children. Evidence of the health crisis is the resurgence of epidemic diseases such as yellow fever, typhoid fever, and guinea worm in both rural and urban centers. The incidence of the diseases of poverty such as rickets, goiter and pellagra is now greater among women than among men.[12]

Newspaper reports describe families consuming food residues formerly fed to domestic animals, and women scouring dust bins and refuse dumps for food and other items. It is common for children to be seen scraping the food plates used at social gatherings for the remnants.

Reports indicate that 50% of children admitted to teaching hospitals in Nigeria are suffering from malnutrition. Comparisons of height for age (anthropometric ratios) of children between 1968 and 1988 confirm this picture. From 0 to 6 months of age, the mean height of children was 11% to 16% lower in 1988 than it was in 1968, and by the age of five years mean height is still 2.5% lower.[13]

CONCLUSION

There is ample evidence that the SAP package has worsened the health of vulnerable groups in Nigeria, notably women and their children. Even though the Federal Military Government embarked on the implementation of PHC in 1986 with an emphasis on maternal and child health, to date little has been done to improve the health of the targeted population even in the first 30 model LGAs, not to mention other "willing" LGAs. The PHC focuses principally on health education, nutrition immunization, prenatal care, and family planning programs. Some LGAs have immunization, prenatal care, and family planning programs. Some LGAs have not even activated proposals to enable them to get their share of the money earmarked for the program. In 1989, the federal government came out with a population policy of four children for every Nigerian mother. But improvement in the health of mothers and in child survival are imperative if this policy is to have any meaning for women. The health of children is now too poor for women to think of family planning, bearing in mind that the majority still have no access to it.

Adherence to the SAP package must be reexamined in order to maintain basic infrastructure and health care services for the general population, women and children in particular. If this is not done, the country is likely to pay the price of physical and mental ill-health for generations to come. In attempting to pay back our debts, we cannot afford to put our future population in jeopardy. There is a need to introduce a "human face" into an adjustment program by targeting vulnerable groups so that their problems are not compounded.

NOTES

1. *Bulletin* (Lagos: Central Bank of Nigeria, 1987); *Annual Report and Statement of Accounts,* (Lagos: Central Bank of Nigeria, 1989).
2. B.O. Osuntokun, "Health Delivery and Management in a Teaching Hospital in Tropical Africa," Erionosho O.A. and Akindele M.O. (eds), *Health Care and Health Services in Nigeria* (African Development Foundation, 1987).
3. J. Ohiorhunan, O. Erionosho, and B. Iyun; *Some Financial Aspects of the Health Care Delivery System in Oyo State, Nigeria* (World Bank, 1985).
4. Folasade Iyun, *Process Documentation and Evaluation Study of the Ogbomoso Community Health Care Programme* (Ford Foundation, West Africa, 1988).

5. H. Ukwu and B. Nwakoby, "State Health Institutions in Amambra State," Ohiorhunan et al., *Financial Aspects.*
6. S. Saba. "Health Care Services in Niger State", M.J. Ohiorhunan, et al., (1985).
7. *Ibid.*
8. Osuntokun,"Health Delivery and Management."
9. *Medical Records,* University College Hospital (Ibadan: 1989).
10. Iyun, *Process Documentation.*
11. Osuntokun, "Health Delivery and Management."
12. *Ibid.*
13. K. Osinusi and C. Oyejide, "Secular Trends in Nutritional Status of Children from a Low Socio-economic Background", *Nigerian Journal of Paediatrics* 14, no. 1 (1987).

CHAPTER FOUR

STRUCTURAL ADJUSTMENT AND FEMALE WAGE LABOR IN THE NIGERIAN TEXTILE INDUSTRY

Adebayo and Hussainatu Olukoshi

The Nigerian economy is currently in the throes of a major crisis of accumulation, the most serious to be experienced by the state since its inception in the early years of this century. The crisis, which was first officially acknowledged in April 1983 with a set of austerity measures, was triggered by the collapse of the world oil market on which Nigeria depended for over 80% of its foreign exchange earnings.[1] The crisis has resulted in the sharp decline of agricultural and industrial production, an ever-rising rate of inflation, the mass retrenchment of workers, the collapse of consumer purchasing power, a massive external debt burden, persistent balance-of-payments difficulties, chronic deficits in the annual federal budget, and the decay of physical and social infrastructure, among other consequences.

In a bid to contain the economic crisis, the government of

General Ibrahim Babangida decided in July 1986, under a great deal of pressure from the International Monetary Fund (IMF) and the World Bank, to introduce a comprehensive program of structural adjustment (SAP) to provide the framework for recovery and growth.[2] Although SAP was a logical outcome of the previous efforts at adjustment made by the Shagari (1979–1983) and Buhari (1983–1985) administrations, it differed significantly from earlier economic recovery programs in its emphasis on the forces of the market.[3] Indeed, at the heart of SAP is an exchange-rate-led economic recovery strategy in which the devaluation of the Nigerian Naira (N) is central. Through the devaluation of the Naira, it is hoped that the huge Nigerian appetite for all manner of imports (raw materials, spare parts, machinery, and consumer goods) will be checked. Industry will be encouraged to source its inputs locally and local value-added tax will thus be raised. Also, devaluation is expected to lead to a resurgence in agricultural production through higher incomes for the peasantry. Increased agricultural production should in turn assist Nigeria to diversify its export base and reduce the country's food import bill and near total reliance on oil as the chief foreign exchange earner. Foreign investment flows to the country should also be enhanced. Taken together with other measures such as the deregulation of interests and prices, the removal of subsidies, the privatization and commercialization of public enterprises, the liberalization of trade, and the removal of bureaucratic controls, the devaluation of the Naira was expected to lay the basis for a more balanced, inward-looking economic order in Nigeria.[4]

STRUCTURAL ADJUSTMENT PROGRAMS AND THE NIGERIAN TEXTILE INDUSTRY

Yet, in practice, years after the introduction of SAP, most of the benefits which were supposed to accrue to the economy from the program are yet to be realized. The industrial sector, for example, is still characterized by decline and under capacity utilization, especially among those firms that are heavily import-dependent for their inputs. But even among those firms that obtain their raw materials locally, capacity utilization is still very low in part because the rigid fiscal policies that have been associated with SAP have had the combined effect of drastically reducing the purchasing power of Nigerians, thereby creating a serious problem of realization for industry. Similarly, the credit and liquidity squeeze introduced by the government in a bid to check the inflationary consequences of devaluation has led to serious cash flow problems for many companies.

Matters have not been helped by the high interest rates occasioned by SAP. The domestic decline in the value of the Naira from almost 1:1 to the British pound sterling (£) in 1985 to about N15:£1 in January 1988, and N23:£1 in 1992, has had the adverse effect of killing many small-scale and medium-scale firms while even the bigger companies have found that the cost of remaining in business is very high indeed.[5]

The Nigerian textile industry, which by 1980 was the third largest in Africa, surpassed only by Egypt and South Africa and boasting some 100 factories and 100,000 workers, has been particularly hard hit by the adjustment policies of the state. This is because in the course of the late 1970s, the industry became heavily dependent on imported raw materials. This should not be surprising as the 1970s, when Nigeria's oil exports reached their peak, was a period of all-around decline in the country's agricultural sector.[6] As with other agricultural raw materials, domestic cotton production in the country underwent a gradual decline, compelling the textile mills (unable to obtain foreign exchange to procure the inputs they needed for production) to close down in large numbers over varying periods of time, victims of their own dependence on external sources of raw materials supply. Various aspects of the Babangida administration's SAP did not help matters. If anything, the industry was placed under even greater strain, characterized by further closures and a shortening of the working day and week.[7]

It is a mark of the seriousness of the crisis in the textile industry and the unemployment effects of SAP on it that by 1987, from a figure of 100,000 in 1980, only about 55,000 workers were still employed. This represents a decline of 45% in the workforce employed in the industry. Membership in the National Union of Textile, Garment and Tailoring Workers of Nigeria (NUTGTWN) sank from 70,000 at the end of 1980 to about 40,000 in the middle of 1987. In addition to the tens of thousands of textile workers who were laid off, the level of capacity utilization in the industry was generally low, ranging from 30% to 45% for much of the period from 1983 to 1987. Many textile mills were forced to reduce the number of shifts they ran from three to one in some cases while others sent many workers on compulsory leave pending the acquisition of an appreciable amount of raw materials. The collapse in consumer purchasing power following the drastic devaluation of the Naira created a serious problem of realization for the textile industry as the market for textiles shrank and manufacturers were stuck with their products in warehouses all over the country.[8]

STRUCTURAL ADJUSTMENT PROGRAMS AND THE NIGERIAN FEMALE TEXTILE WORKERS

If, as we have argued, SAP has, in its consequences, led to a general decline in the Nigerian textile industry, what has this meant for female wage labor in the female subsector of the economy? This is a crucial question, given that female wage labor in industry in Nigeria is still a relatively new phenomenon. The employment of female wage labor is certainly not a common feature of the Nigerian industrial scene, limited as it is to companies mostly engaged in the production of sweets and confectioneries, soaps, perfumes, and other toiletries, and textile materials. With this fact in mind, we conducted interviews in some of the leading textile mills in Lagos (Nigeria's leading industrial and commercial center), with the aim of finding out if SAP has, at least in the case of the textile industry, led to a temporary set-back in the process of proletarianization of women. We also wanted to know if there was any evidence that employers in the textile industry were generally quicker to retrench female workers than their male colleagues. If the evidence suggested that women were more likely to be retrenched before men, we wanted to know the reason for this.[9]

Table 1 summarizes aspects of the results of interviews conducted among 11 textile companies in Lagos in September 1988.

Eight of the companies were established between 1969 and 1971, Atlantic Textile being the only one established before 1969 while the Nigerian Embroidery Lace Manufacturing Company and K. Issaradas Limited were set up in 1974 and 1986, respectively. Nine of the firms started production with a total workforce of 100 or less, with five of these employing 50 workers or less at the time they started business. Only Nigerian Synthetic Fibres Limited and Bhojsons Industries Limited employed over 100 workers each, the latter starting production with a labor force of 450, which qualifies it as one of the biggest textile mills in the country in the early 1970s. The remaining firms could accurately be described as small-scale and medium-scale factories at the time they started production, although Table 1 does contain evidence to suggest that some of them recorded dramatic growths in their sizes as demonstrated by the large increases in their labor forces.

Each of the 11 firms covered in the survey had women in their workforce from the time they went into production. Seven of the companies employed 20 female workers or less at the time they started business while the remaining four employed over 20 workers each, although only Dalmalal Limited had up to 50 women in its workforce at its inception. It is clear from Table 1, and Table 2 illustrates even more graphically, that women were a minority of the labor force in the companies surveyed, a trend which is most certainly equally true for the rest of the textile industry and the Nigerian manufacturing sector as a whole. In most of the firms, women formed less than 40% of the workforce, with Bhojson's Industries Limited and Fablon Industries Limited having the least proportion of female employees relative to their total labor force. Only two companies, Haffer Industries Limited and Dalmalal Limited, started business with women accounting for up to half of their employees, the majority of the women employed on the shop floor as weavers, knitters, folders, and seamstresses. Nigerian Synthetic Fabrics reported women as machine operators while Dalmalal had two women working as nurses, and four others as administrative junior staff. Significantly, none of the companies had women in junior or senior management positions.

As can be seen from Table 1, there is evidence to suggest that there was, over the years from the start of production to the end of August, 1988, an increase, in absolute terms, in the number of women employed by a majority of the 11 companies surveyed. For example, even with the severe crisis facing the industry, six of the 11 companies still have more female workers in their employment at the end of 31 August 1988 than when they first started production. Also, of the eight firms that reported that they had to lay off women in response to the crisis and the difficulties created for them by SAP, five retrenched more female workers than the number they started production with, while the remaining three sacked almost an equal number of women as those they recruited at the time they opened for business. Still, the evidence suggests an increase in the number of women employed notwithstanding. It is also clear from Table 1 that the rate of growth of female wage labor recruitment into the companies was generally low with the consequence that women were unable by 31 August 1988 to sustain the percentage-share of the workforce which they held at the time the survey companies started production. A close comparison of Tables 2 and 3 brings this out graphically. Only one company, Haffer Industries Limited, had women accounting for a percentage share of its 1988 total workforce higher than when it started business. For the remaining ten companies, there was a drastic fall in the proportion of jobs held by women. Indeed, none had female workers accounting for up to a full 10% of its workforce at the end of 31 August 1988.

Why is it that women were unable to sustain the proportion of jobs which they held in the survey companies in the period between the time the firms started production and 31 August 1988? Clearly, as noted earlier, Table 1 offers ample evidence that many of the firms underwent rapid expansion processes which women should ordinarily have benefitted from. It would seem to us that two factors account for the reduction in the rate of growth of female wage labor in the 11 textile mills. First, it seems very probable that as the companies grew in size, many of the firms tended to recruit more male workers than female, with the consequence that the percentage share of the labor force held by women when the companies started production was not retained. The only probable exception was Haffer Industries Limited, in which women constituted almost 70% of the workforce at the end of August, 1988. Second, as a result of the economic crisis of the 1980s in Nigeria, and also because of the adverse effects of SAP on the textile industry, a greater proportion of women relative to their size was retrenched by the employers. Certainly, the evidence from Tables 1 and 4 seems to suggest that a good number of the eight firms that reported that they retrenched workers were apparently more inclined to lay off a proportionally higher number of women than men. For instance, of the 16 workers sacked by Haffer Industries Company Limited, 83% consisted of women in various grades. Similarly, 75% of those sacked by Dalalmal Limited were women. Women also made up over 50% of the workers laid off by Nigerian Synthetic Fabrics Limited and K. Issadras Limited. For Jay Bee Limited and Fablon Industries Limited, it was 32% and 20%, respectively.

The evidence we have presented in Table 4 is particularly significant for the reason that women who were, from the outset, a minority of the workforce in the 11 survey companies and who, as the firms grew, tended to lose their proportional share of jobs to men, seemed also to be more likely to be retrenched by their employers as a result of the effects of the economic crisis and the problems created by SAP for the textile industry. Even Haffer Industries Limited which, as we noted earlier, appeared to be the only firm that increased the percentage-share of women in its workforce, also recorded the highest percentage-share of women retrenched in relation to the total workforce. Indeed, the number of women laid off by higher than the total number of women employed by the firm as a proportion of its total labor force in 1969 when it started production and as at the end of August 1988.

If, as the evidence suggests, women have fared badly in the textile industry and appeared to be more likely to lose their jobs before their male counterparts, we sought to find out why this was so by asking the managers of the 11 survey companies what they thought of the productivity of women in relation to men and vice versa. Significantly, the managers of seven of the companies held the view that women, as gender groups, were generally less productive than men. Among the reasons given by the managers for this view is the "family obligations" of women — that is, women tend to require too much time to attend to family problems, the most frequently mentioned being the need to attend to sick children. Some of the managers also note that the women in their workforce were generally less skilled than the men and did not show the "required aptitude" for acquiring new skills. Furthermore, some the managers said that their female workers seemed to be more prone to absenteeism than the male workers and tended to ask for sick leave more frequently than the men.

Equally significant is the fact that only two of the managers of the 11 survey companies felt that women were as productive as men. In support of their view, they noted that the women in their employment performed their functions very well, as well as or sometimes even better than the men employed in the same jobs. If they had occasion to retrench women as indeed both of them did, it was not because they were less productive but because the dictates of the SAP made this inevitable. The acute shortage of raw materials faced by the textile mills made it necessary for them to prune their labor force.

As to the two remaining companies, their managers took the position that the productivity of their female wage-labor force relative to that of the men varied from section to section. In some sections of their textile mills (in particular, the sewing, weaving, and knitting sections), the women workers were clearly more productive than their male counterparts while in others like the packing and spinning sections, the men were more productive.

Given that the managers of seven out of the eleven companies surveyed believe that women generally are less productive than men, it is perhaps not surprising that the majority of the firms not only slowed down their recruitment of female workers after they started production but also retrenched a high ratio of their women laborers. There is certainly a case to be made for the argument that there is an organic linkage between the gender bias of an all-male management team and the high level of redundancy declared among female workers in the textile firms surveyed. Thus, although the adversities brought on the textile industry by the Nigerian economic crisis and the adjustment program of the state were an important factor in the retrenchment of women workers, it is sustainable to argue that gender discrimination did contribute to the relatively high level of redundancies suffered by the women and the slowing down by the managers of the recruitment of female laborers even before the onset of the crisis in the textile industry.

It is interesting to note that almost all of the women retrenched by the eight firms that reported having laid off female workers belong to the active working population in Nigeria. As Table 5 shows, in seven out of the eight firms, the women who were retrenched were in the 20- to 40-year age range, a fact that underscores the relative youthfulness of the female labor force and enables us to imagine how negative the effects of being made redundant could have been for the affected women. Bhojson's Industries Limited was the only company that reported that most of its retrenched female workers fell in the 40- to 50-year age bracket, the most notable exception being a 60-year old woman who also lost her job with the company.

CONCLUDING REMARKS

It is clear from the evidence we obtained from the 11 companies surveyed that Nigerian women employed in the textile industry have been adversely affected by the repercussions arising from the state's adoption of an IMF/World Bank adjustment program. It would seem that the crisis in the textile industry has had the effect of, at least temporarily, slowing down the rate of proletarianization of women in that subsector of the economy. It is equally evident that the greater vulnerability of women to retrenchment in the industry bears a close relationship to gender discrimination, which discrimination also accounts for the decline in their percentage share of jobs in the textile companies surveyed. Thus, the economic crisis in Nigeria and the structural adjustment policy of the government have affected female laborers in the textile industry at two levels—as workers, and as women. As various textile companies, in response to the dictates of SAP, begin to source their raw materials locally by going into cotton farming, it is likely that the industry will begin to witness an increase, however marginal, in its labor requirements and output. [10] What is not certain, however, is that women will benefit in any meaningful way from any upturn in the industry.

Table 1.
Summary of effects of SAP-related retrenchment among female wage-labor subsector of Nigerian textile industry.

Name of Company	A*	B	C	D	E	F	G
Haffer Industries Ltd.	1969	48	24	209	140	66	55
Nigerian Weaving and Processing Company Ltd.	1971	50	7	257	15	59	NIL
Nigerian Synthetic Fabrics Ltd.	1969	140	44	339	14	1261	700
Bhojsons Industries Ltd.	1971	450	12	1088	67	254	11
Five Star Industries Ltd.	1969	60	20	1591	82	508	18
Dalmalal Limited	1971	100	50	338	4	120	90
Jay Bee Limited	1969	59	29	150	10	400	130
K. Issaradas Limited	1986	50	15	140	1	25	NIL
Nigerian Embroidery Lace Manufacturing Company	1974	100	46	317	22	97	NIL
Atlantic Textile Manufacturing Ltd.	1965	60	12	573	40	NIL	NIL
Fablon Industries Ltd.	1969	42	2	517	48	70	14

*A.   year of establishment
B.   total no. of workers (male and female) started with
C.   total no. of female workers started with
D.   no. of employees (male and female) as at 31.8.88
E.   no. of female workers as at 31.8.88
F.   no. of workers (male and female) retrenched due to present crisis
G.   no. of female workers retrenched due to present crisis

Source: interviews conducted by the authors in Lagos in September 1988.

Table 2.
Women as a percentage of the total workforce
at start of production

Company	% women
Haffer Industries Limited	50.0
Nigerian Weaving and Processing Company Limited	14.0
Nigerian Synthetic Fabrics Limited	31.4
Bhojsons Industries Limited	2.6
Dalmalal Limited	50.0
Jay Lee Limited	40.0
K. Issaradas Limited	30.0
Nigerians Embroidery Lace Manufacturing Company	46.0
Atlantic Textiles Manufacturing	20.0
Fablon Industries Limited	4.7
Five Star Industries Limited	33.3

Source: Interviews conducted by the authors in
Lagos in September 1988.

Table 3.
Women as a percentage of the total workforce
as of 31 August 1988

Company	% women
Haffer Industries Limited	67.0
Nigerian Weaving and Processing Company Limited	5.8
Nigerian Synthetic Fabrics Limited	4.1
Bhojsons Industries Limited	6.1
Dalmalal Limited	5.1
Jay Lee Limited	6.6
K. Issaradas Limited	0.7
Nigerians Embroidery Lace Manufacturing Company	7.0
Atlantic Textiles Manufacturing	7.0
Fablon Industries Limited	9.2
Five Star Industries Limited	1.1

Source: Interviews conducted by the authors in
Lagos in September, 1988.

Table 4.
Women workers retrenched as a percentage of the
total workforce retrenched in Nigerian textile industry.

Company	% women
Haffer Industries Limited	83.3
Nigerian Weaving and Processing Company Limited	nil
Nigerian Synthetic Fabrics Limited	55.5
Bhojsons Industries Limited	4.3
Dalmalal Limited	75.0
Jay Lee Limited	32.5
K. Issaradas Limited	52.0
Nigerians Embroidery Lace Manufacturing Company	nil
Atlantic Textiles Manufacturing	nil
Fablon Industries Limited	20.0
Five Star Industries Limited	3.5

Source: Interviews conducted by the authors in Lagos in September,
1988.

Table 5.
Age range of women retrenched by
textile companies in Lagos

Company	Age 20-30 yrs	Age 30-40 yrs	Age 40-50 yrs
Haffer Industries Limited		x	
Nigerian Synthetic Fabric Limited		x	
Bhojsons Industries Limited			x
Dalmalal Limited		x	
Jay Lee Limited	x		
K. Issaradas Limited		x	
Fablon Industries Limited	x		
Five Star Industries Limited	x		

Source: Interviews conducted by the authors in Lagos in September,
1988.

NOTES

1. In April 1983, the Shagari administration introduced the Economic Stabilization (Emergency Powers) Act in its effort to check the escalating crisis in the Nigerian economy. Since then, there has been a great deal of debate in Nigeria on the actual causes of the crisis. Is the crisis simply the result of the collapse of the world oil market or are there deeper, underlying structural distortions in the economy which the world oil market glut simply helped to expose? Perhaps the most celebrated academic exchange on the cause of the crisis is the one between Yusuf Bangura and Yusufu Bala Usman which has now been published under the title "Debate on the Nigerian Economic Crisis" as a Special Issue of *Politics and Society*, No. 2 (1984).
2. *Structural Adjustment Program* (Lagos: Government Printer, 1986).
3. A. Olukoshi, Debt-Equity Conversion as an Instrument of Structural Adjustment in Nigeria: A Critique, in A. Olukoshi, ed., *The Nigerian External Debt Crisis: Its Management* (Lagos and Oxford: Malthouse Press, 1989).
4. S. P. Okongwu, *One Year of Structural Adjustment in Nigeria: An Assessment*. (Lagos: Government Printer, 1987).
5. *Annual Report* (Lagos: Central Bank of Nigeria, 1987).
6. *Ibid.*
7. Yusuf Bangura, *Structural Adjustment and De-industrialization in Nigeria*, (mimeo) (1987).
8. Gunilla Andrae and Bjorn Beckman, *Industry Goes Farming: The Nigerian Raw Material Crisis and the Case of Textiles and Cotton.* (Uppsala: SIAS, 1987a)
9. G. Andrae and B. Beckman, *Workers' Power and the Crisis of the Nigerian Textile Industry.* (mimeo) (1987).
10. G. Andrae and B. Beckman, *Report on Research on Kaduna Textiles Limited Workers.* (Zaria, 1987b); also Y. Bangura and Yusufu Bala Usman, "Debate on the Nigerian Economic Crisis" in *Politics and Society.* 2 (1984).

CHAPTER FIVE

CRISIS AND STRUCTURAL ADJUSTMENT IN SIERRA LEONE: IMPLICATIONS FOR WOMEN*

A. Zack-Williams

The past two decades have witnessed a gradual decline in the fortunes of the Sierra Leone state and the erosion of the standard of living of the vast majority of its population. The impact of the crisis and the capacity to cope with it varies from one social group to another. The most vulnerable groups have tended to be the urban poor, children, women, and old people living off their savings or on fixed incomes (in 1986, inflation was running at over 171%). The role of women in Sierra Leone society has meant that they bear the brunt of the crisis and of the 'corrective actions' of the International Monetary Fund (IMF) and the World Bank stabilization and adjustment policies.

In this chapter, I want to look at the nature of the crisis, at attempts by the Sierra Leone authorities to deal with it, at the impact of the crisis on women, and at their various survival strategies.

Locating The Crisis:
Its Nature and Causal Factors

Between 1950-1972, Sierra Leone experienced an average annual growth rate of 7%. This was accompanied by rising incomes in the agricultural, mining, and manufacturing sectors. During this period agriculture and mining remained the cornerstones of economic performance, particularly in the export sector. Between 1960 and 1970, agriculture accounted for 33% of gross domestic product (GDP) and mining accounted for 18%. In 1969 diamonds accounted for 69% of the value of total exports. Inflation averaged below 5% annually. There were low balance-of-payment deficits and budget deficits. The period was also marked by large scale infrastructural investments by the government, as part of its open door policy designed to attract foreign capital.

However, the growth rate began to slow down in the mid 1970s and from 1980 the economy went into a nose dive. The annual growth rate fell to 5.6% between 1980-85.

External factors include the oil-price increases after 1973 and worsening terms of trade after 1975, with a steady fall in the price of major exports. For example, between 1977 and 1986 the price of cocoa fell from £3,000 to £600. There was also a decline in the volume of cocoa, palm kernels, and diamond exports. In 1986 diamonds accounted for only 39% of exports, dropping from 2 million carats in 1970 to a derisory 48,000 carats in 1988. This fall was due partly to the depletion of alluvial deposits and partly to the government's inability to control smuggling.

Internal causes of the downturn are closely linked to the external. Low producer prices for export crops have intensified smuggling to neighboring countries where the US$ or CFA franc are legal tender. Economic mismanagement and corruption have intensified. This is closely related to the lack of accountability.[1] Overdependence on imported goods reflected the failure of the import-substitution strategy and was a drain on precious foreign exchange. Long-term debt stood at $695 million by 1987, more than five times the recorded exports of goods and services for that year.

Prior to 1986, government response can be characterized as "business as usual," i.e., it ran up relatively large unbudgeted deficits using external loans to finance them. Between 1977 and 1985 a number of ad hoc rescheduling agreements were signed with the Paris Club, as well as supporting programs from the IMF to overcome balance-of-payments problems. In November 1986 the first long term structural adjustment facility with the IMF was concluded. It was supposed to last for three years and the Fund agreed to a standby credit of SDR 40.53 million in return for the following conditionalities:

1. Reduction in the size of the bureaucracy, and limits on the growth of government expenditures
2. Removal of subsidies on essential commodities such as petroleum and rice
3. Deregulation of the importation of rice
4. Liberalization of the exchange rate
5. Institutionalization of a market-determined exchange rate to eliminate the parallel market in foreign currency
6. Decontrol retail trade
7. Increases in the producer prices for major cash crops
8. Rationalization of the mining sector, and its privatization
9. Simplification of the tax system, and deregulation of interest rates
10. Devaluation of the currency (which took place in June 1986, in anticipation of the signing of the agreement)

The recurrent budget deficit between 1980 and 1989 was due partly to an inflated bureaucracy, fueled by the client-patron relationship upon which politics is based. For example, when the IMF insisted that the wage bill be reduced by 40% in the year 1988/89, this was achieved without any significant rise in unemployment. The return of 'ghost workers' the following year saw budget overspending within six months.

The agreement was, however, suspended by the IMF in April 1987, after only SDR 11.58 million of the loan had been used.

This was because of what the Fund saw as poor performance, in particular, failure to depreciate the currency fast enough and accumulated arrears owing to the Fund. In January 1988 both parties agreed to a 'shadow program' which never materialized because the government was fearful of the social and economic consequences of devaluing the currency by 100%. Further meetings finally led to an agreement and in April 1990 the government started to implement some conditionalities, devaluing the currency by floatation, decontrolling interest rates, and liberalizing trade.

The Social Costs

Currently, savings have been wiped out by inflation. Development expenditure has suffered, accounting for only 7.6% of total expenditure in the first six months of 1989/90. Social and economic infrastructure is at breaking point: schools, hospitals, and clinics have been left to decay while the private sector charges prices well beyond the means of the average wage-earner.

Health workers, teachers, and civil servants have to go for months without salaries, leading to demoralization which further affects their services. Most turn to the informal sector (the 'second economy') to supplement their income. This is true of professionals as well as daily-wage earners. Resources such as drugs, books, and other equipments destined for the state sector are often diverted to the private sector by corrupt officials and politicians. State hospitals have a permanent shortage of essential drugs which are readily available in private clinics or drug stores, a large number of which are owned by politicians or senior health workers. With 300 doctors in the country (including 42 who are on leave and may never return), there is one doctor to every 11,728 persons and one bed to 875 persons.

Urban areas are characterized by overcrowding, malnutrition, poor sanitation, squalid dwellings, chronic electricity failure, environmental pollution, and irregular water supply, even in the capital city. These are all problems which tend to have more of an impact on women than on any other social category.

The Position of Women

Women do not constitute a homogeneous social category. Like men, they are differentiated along class, ethnic, and regional lines. These determine the position in which a particular woman finds herself. For instance, rural women and poor urban women will have different mechanism for copying with the crisis.

Nonetheless, there are certain features that women in Sierra Leone share in common to the extent that they are not remunerated for their domestic efforts, neither for biological reproduction nor for their major responsibility for the welfare of current and future producers. In this context we can argue that women as a group are 'over-exploited' within African social formation.[2]

Childbearing begins relatively early in Sierra Leone. Sixteen percent of all children are born to mothers 19 years of age or under. Sixty percent of women marry by the age of 20. The total parity rate is 6.5 children per women.[3] This increases the risk of early mortality.

As far as educational indices are concerned, 77% of women over 15 years of age have no formal education, and only 15% of girl pupils reach secondary school. As UNICEF noted:

> As women carry a double load, as both farmers and domestic workers, they have little time or energy for educational programs. The dry season between harvest and sowing, the 'slack season', when women might be expected to have time for such classes, is also the time chosen by secret societies for their ritual activities, and villagers are afraid to be out at night on these occasions.[4]

In 1989, UNICEF estimated that Sierra Leonean women worked an average of 16 hours a day "either in the home, in the fields or walking as far as eight miles a day to fetch wood, food, or water." In spite of using so much energy, the report noted that the majority of women ate only one meal a day, and only 5% could afford three meals a day. Twenty percent suffered from anemia, and this rose to 30% among pregnant women. Not surprisingly, maternal mortality is 700 per 1,000, — i.e., 70% — due mainly to anemia, malnutrition, and infections.

In the rural areas a woman is still seen as the 'chattel' of her husband. Her bondage is legitimized by the 'dowry': a woman can be divorced at the behest of her husband, but if she decides to leave him she must return the dowry.

As domestic managers, women tend to use the help of children, though urban women, particularly from the urban petty bourgeoisie use outside labour. In the southern part of the country, where Islam holds less sway, there are politically influential women who, as well as employing male workers, hold chieftaincy titles.[5] In this area gender specialization is not hard and fast. By contrast, in the northern part, where Islam is strong, women cannot hold political office, nor do they have control over the labor of men. Most petty traders are women, and most come from the North. Women prepare and market 95% of the smoke-dried fish consumed in the country. UNICEF estimated that between 60% and 80% of agricultural work was performed by women, though Richards in his study of the Mogbuama in the southern province, noted that:

> I have little evidence that the burdens [of work] fall disproportionately on women and children.... Mogbuama farm households are generally too poor, and too constrained...to permit any major degree of male 'exploitation' of female labour, in the simple sense of male 'leisure' consumed at the expense of female work.

Women and Survival Strategies

A fundamental assumption behind structural adjustment policies, noted by Elson, is the belief that women would continue to provide their services of human reproduction free of charge. Indeed, she cautioned, "Women's unpaid labour is not infinitely elastic — a breaking point may be reached, and women's capacity to reproduce and maintain human resources may collapse."[6]

The crisis, and the subsequent 'correctional' policies have impacted disproportionately on women. Not only are women expected to continue their "dual labor" as social and biological producers, but these roles have become more burdensome due to inflation, unemployment, running down of social and welfare services. As the traditional carers for the sick, the old, and the young, women's task has become more onerous. In some cases even the direct wage of the "bread winner" has disappeared. Women have to increase their efforts to maintain the family by redoubling their remunerated and nonremunerated tasks.

In many parts of sub-Saharan Africa, husband and wife do not pool resources and do not have a common housekeeping or child-rearing budget.[7] Similarly, in fishing communities in Sierra Leone, women and men keep their capital funds independently and women provide for the greater part of food and household maintenance requirements.[8] Prior to the present crisis, the tradition in many households in Sierra Leone was for an employed woman to bear the financial cost of bringing up the children, including clothing and care. This was supplemented by 'support money' from the husband, who would be responsible for such expenditures as rent, rates, and school fees.

Now, the loss of father's earnings has tended to increase the responsibility of women, but without conferring social power. In short, whilst the crisis has helped to restructure the role of women, within the household, yet women are still subjected to the overall culture of male dominance.[9] Women are emerging as breadwinners but without the social recognition.

The 'support money' has been seriously eroded in real terms. Yet, men expect the same food in their diet. It is left to the women as house managers to make ends meet. The prohibitive price of beef, for instance, has meant that many more families have to depend on fish as a relatively cheap form of protein, though an increasing number are turning to 'bush meat' to supplement fish. In the southern region, Richards noted that the local wild yam (Dioscorea Minutiflora) is an important food item in the 'hungry' season.

The dwindling value of 'support money' is a major source of domestic conflict, with many women threatening not to perform domestic management chores, or asking their husbands to 'try and do the shopping'. In these circumstances women are the ones who tradition expects to make sacrifices. They tend to go without food to help the family. Men must have food, as long as they provide 'chop money.' Children are an even lower priority, and only after they had been fed do women feel they can have their meal. Irregular electricity and water supplies are a source of further frustration to women. Bulk buying in order to beat shortages and inflation often ends up in disaster with entire freezer loads being lost when the power fails.

To supplement the household budget many women now embark on income-generating activities. Even those in full-time work in the formal sector now have second jobs or simply 'moonlight' to make ends meet. Rural women try to stave off hunger by intercropping of both subsistence and cash crops.[10] Sometimes this involves child labor in the preparation and distribution of goods for sale.

These kinds of survival strategies, referred to as 'doing mammy coker,' are quite common among those working in the state sector where stagnant wages and delays in payment have led to demoralization. Many workers treat their jobs with disdain, putting in only a brief appearance before moving on to 'mammy coker'.

There is another survival strategy, known as 'dregg,' a term with worrying connotations and serious gender implications. It is a strategy particularly adopted by young women and takes several forms: carrying out demeaning tasks, begging, acting as 'groupie' to politicians and military officers, and offering casual sexual favors. The proliferation of 'dregg' is indicative of the severe impact of the crisis on women.

Men, the creators of the crisis (by their dominance in political and public life) tend to blame women for aspects of the crisis. Women traders, especially the Hadjas who deal in rice, are often blamed for inflationary prices. This reached crisis point in 1987 when the Chair of the Freetown City Council decided to evacuate traders, from their unofficial roadside markets on the pretext that they were an eyesore in a modern capital. Military precision was used to drive the traders who later succeeded in reversing the decision, partly for ethnic reasons, as the vice president came from the same ethnic group as the women.

Conclusion

In this chapter I have tried to identify the crisis in Sierra Leone and attempts being made to deal with the crisis. I have drawn attention to the effects of the crisis on women and to subsequent adjustment policies and how the symptoms of the crisis tend to impact disproportionately on women. One effect has been to increase the responsibilities of women without affording them any recognition of their new role. Women are still not recognised as breadwinners by the state or employers and, in fact, are blamed for aspects of the crisis.

NOTES

* Field trip for this paper was facilitated by a grant from The Nuffield Foundation. I am most grateful to the Foundation for its generosity.

1. A.B. Zack-Williams, "Sierra Leone: Crisis & Despair," *Review of African Political Economy*, 49, (Dec. 1990): 22–33.
2. A.B. Zack-Williams, "Female Labour and Exploitation Within African Social Formations," in: Women in Nigeria, ed., *Women in Nigeria Today*, (Zed, 1985), pp. 61-67.
3. UNICEF, "The Children & Women of Sierra Leone: An Analysis of Their Situation", vol 1, 1989, Freetown: The Ministry of National Development and Economic Planning and UNICEF.
4. *Ibid.*, p. 75.
5. P. Richards, *Coping With Hunger: Hazard and Experiment in an African Rice-Farming System*, (London: Allen and Unwin, 1986).
6. D. Elson, "The Impact of Structural Adjustment on Women: Concepts and Issues" in B. Onimode, *The IMF, the World Bank and the African Debt*, Vol. 2 The Social and Political Impact, (IFAA & Zed Books, 1989). pp. 56–64.
7. A. Whitehead, "The Politics of Domestic Budgeting," in K. Young, C. Wolkowitz, and R. McCullagh, *Of Marriage and the Market: Women's Subordination in International Perspectives* (CSE Books, 1981), pp. 86–111
8. N. Bowen, "Technological Change Under Economic Crisis: Fishwomen in Sierra Leone" (mimeo), October, 1990.
9. D. Elson and R. Pearson, "The Subordination of Women and the Internationalisation of Factory Production", in Young, et al., pp. 144–166.
10. Richards, *Coping With Hunger*.

CHAPTER SIX

GENDER AND ADJUSTMENT: PICTURES FROM GHANA

Lynne Brydon and Karen Legge

One of the problems singled out in studies of the "effects" of adjustment in a particular area is that of the dimension of time. We, or even the major agents of the purse strings of adjustment, can undertake research into the now, the aftermath of the imposition of policies included in stabilization-and-adjustment packages, but it is extremely difficult to gauge just how adjustment has changed local communities and the lives of women in them. What was it like "before"? Is it now better? ..... or worse? Have things, in fact, changed very much?

Given the problems of assessing change, in August 1990 we embarked on a study of the impacts of adjustment policies in selected areas in Ghana. Both of us had worked in Ghana prior to 1990[1] and it seemed sensible, therefore, to include the areas we knew best in the new research. Brydon had known Avatime since before Ghana's major economic decline which led to the seeking of IMF and World Bank lending, and Legge's knowledge of Antoakrom began when the first phase of the Economic

Recovery Plan (ERP) was just beginning to bite. The bulk of this paper, therefore, focuses on Amedzofe and Antoakrom since these are the areas with which we have the longest association. The emphasis in these sections is descriptive rather than analytical. Our final section, however, is comparative and draws on statistical information from our research in all of the rural areas in which we worked. In contrast with the vastly diverging sets of claims about the "effects" of adjustment in Ghana, on one side the success story which aspires to create from Ghana the first NIC in Sub-Saharan Africa, and on the other side stories of belt-tightening horror, particularly detrimental to women, our own conclusions are rather different: a story of "the same continued..."

Amedzofe

Amedzofe is one of a distinct group of seven villages which constitute the Avatime ethnic group and traditional area[2] in the hills in the central Volta Region, not far from the border with Togo and about 25 miles to the north of Ho, the regional capital. Primarily because of its hilly location, Amedzofe was chosen as the site of a mission station in 1889; it was hoped that the climate (mosquito free) would be conducive to rest and convalescence for overworked missionaries stationed in the plains to the south. With the mission station came a school and a seminary for the training of mission personnel and, although initially only boys went to the school, before the end of the German colonial period (the First World War), girls were also being taught to read and write in addition to being taught various aspects of domestic science by the missionaries' wives.

Amedzofe is not rich in natural resources, but from the early years of the century it began to export labor, both educated/ literate labor for the bureaucracies of the Gold Coast and skilled manual labor (also a legacy of the German colonial period). Amedzofe maintained its position as a center for education (particularly teacher training) through the 1970s and its Training College has been recognized as a center for teacher training in the education reforms of the postadjustment years. Brydon showed that in 1974, more than half of men and women in their 20s and early 30s were working away, but in the later 30s and into the 40s increasing proportions of Amedzofe women and men were in the village, the proportion of women being more than that of the men. Although a significant proportion (22%) of the migrant women consisted of teachers (mainly at primary level), reflecting the strong emphasis on education in the village, the range of jobs for women was quite restricted.[3] Migration for women as well as men, in both cases for economic reasons, was a commonplace and in fact seemed to have become the norm at a particular stage in life.[4]

In 1990, the Amedzofe sample had the highest rate of outmigration of all our research sites: mean household size was 13.2 when migrants were included and 7.0, excluding migrants.[5] (There were 660 people in the Amedzofe sample, of whom 308 were away.) But even with these relatively high rates of outmigration the opportunities for earning away from home have diminished both in the informal and the formal sectors. The diminution in opportunities for formal sector employment (the state bureaucracies, teaching) is a direct result of the government's adjustment policies, while the problems in the informal sector seem to be largely the result of overcrowding as more and more workers are forced into it because of the shrinkage in the formal sector.[6] Both men and women are obviously affected here.

Of those who are in Amedzofe, the largest category rely on farming for their livelihoods (45% men and 55% women: see Table 1). Women in Amedzofe have access to land in their own right, whether they are married or not. If they are married (or widowed) they may farm both on their husbands' plots and on plots from their natal families (descent and inheritance in Avatime is patrilineal), but divorced women farm on land from their natal families. Most farming land within the Amedzofe area is not individually owned, but family land is formally distributed at the beginning of the farming season each year so that every entitled (by descent, not gender) person receives a share. To date, there has been no case where a land allocation has been insufficient for a family's needs, but this is at the expense of shortening of fallow periods from a minimum of 15 years to 7 years now[7] with obvious consequences for the long-term viability of farming in the area. Unlike the nearby valley area of Tsito, described by Jette Bukh in 1979, this is not an area where cocoa does well and so the situation of men having the best land for cocoa while women are pushed to marginal land to grow subsistence crops has not arisen. In Amedzofe, women and men grow subsistence crops and any surplus may be sold, either in the small village market each evening or on market days, or, if there is enough produce to warrant the journey, women may headload produce to sell in the rural wholesale market at Logba Alakpeti, a 2- to 3-hour walk away, down the stony mountain paths. Local knowledge of land is such that everyone knows which crops will do well in which areas and plans her/his farms accordingly.

Cocoa is grown by Amedzofe people but now it is largely a legacy from the past. What little cocoa there was around Amedzofe was destroyed by the bush fires of 1983 and has not been replaced in spite of government rhetoric. One of the "classic" migration patterns in the area from the 1920s to 50s was for a young man to go away either to earn enough money to buy a cocoa farm (in the cocoa-growing areas to the north of Hohoe) outright, or to go direct to the cocoa growing areas to work as a share cropper with the aim of securing ownership over at least a part of the farm.[8] While this first generation of cocoa farmers was male, the current constitution of its descendants is both male and female. What little income there is from cocoa in the village is thus not in the control of men only.

Formal efforts at "development" in Amedzofe have been minimal and mainly directed at men. Amedzofe and other Avatime villages were the site of a weaving enterprise (broadloom cloth for uniforms and hand towels) during the Second World War, but this foundered when trade picked up again after the war. Potatoes for the expatriate community in Accra were also grown in Amedzofe during the war, but again production foundered when imports became available. In 1976 some Amedzofe men formed a cooperative to produce and market potatoes in Accra. The group secured a loan to buy a tractor, seed potatoes, and some fertilizer and pesticide. Marketing was to be carried out through one of the group's relatives working for "Kingsway" stores in Accra and in late 1976 a bus arrived to transport the potato crop to Accra. With the demise of the tractor, however, and failure to reinvest in the infrastructure, the enterprise dwindled after about two years.

For as long as the oldest generation can remember, and in their mothers' and grandmothers' times, Amedzofe women have always had independent sources of income. While Amedzofe men were trying to make money from cocoa growing in the 1940s and 50s, Amedzofe women were renowned as fruit growers and traders, in particular, of bananas and oranges. From the 40s to the 60s Amedzofe women were, apparently, regular visitors at periodic markets all over the southern part of the Volta region. Through the late 60s and 70s this trade dwindled as Ghana's economy declined, not because women did not need to earn or were denied access to the fruit, but because the obstacles to selling were so great. A specific example will suffice.

In July 1979, during the Nigerian/ Western imposed oil embargo in Ghana, three Amedzofe women decided to try to sell bananas outside of the area so that they could at least pay their children's school fees and buy their school uniforms. After spending two days collecting the green bananas, one of the women headloaded a basketful of bananas to the nearest market town on its market day both to sell the bananas and to arrange transport for a lorry-load of bananas out of Amedzofe. The "lorry" (a small Datsun pickup) was due to arrive in the village at dawn the following day to take the bananas to Ho, the regional capital. The lorry arrived at about 9:30 A.M., loaded the bananas and the women and filled vacant space with fare-paying passengers and their luggage. Because of the late start the bananas arrived in Ho too late to be sold to the major wholesale buyers (it was not Ho market day), but one small advantage was that because it was so late, the soldiers who had been overseeing the fair-price selling of wholesale produce had left. The Amedzofe women could sell their fruit at what they thought was a good price, but the buyers were slow in coming. The lorry driver, having deemed his part of the bargain over, took his money and fares and left without taking the women back up the mountain to the village. One woman's share of the profits was enough to enable her to visit some relatives in the south and to buy a blouse for herself and cloth for uniforms for her children. The opinion of the women was that the driver had grossly over-charged them, but that if they wanted to sell anything at all they had to take his offer: they had no choice. The problems of trans-port out of the village during the later years of decline were such that villagers, both as passengers and traders, could be effec-tively held for ransom by the owners and drivers of vehicles. In Amedzofe this situation was exacerbated because the steep mountain tracks had fallen into such a state of disrepair. Many owners were reluctant to risk their vehicles on bad roads when all spare parts had to be brought in (usually illegally) from out-side the country.

Before the 1980s, therefore, women's attempts at "development" were on an individual basis. Women struggled to earn cash to contribute to family incomes.[9] Everyone was liable for and con-tributed communal labor when required, but communal labor tended to be concentrated on weeding the roadsides and gener-ally tidying up the village before the visit of someone important or a special occasion such as Easter.[10] During the 80s, however, some Amedzofe women have become involved in community development projects, first, together with men, in the building of a Health Post (staffed by government nurses but funded partly from church and mission sources) and second, through the 31st December Women's Movement they have provided labor for an intermittent potato-growing enterprise, but this has failed because of a poor growing season in the late 1980s and the inability either to generate enough potatoes for seed or money to buy in new seed potatoes. Like the men earlier, the women had received advice from the local field officer of the Agricultural Extension Service, but this was limited and did not extend to practical help.

Until the end of the 1980s, therefore, Amedzofe women had not been involved in any externally financed development pro-ject, either through the government or a nongovernmental orga-nization. However, included in the government's postadjustment package of remedial programs, the Programme of Actions to Mitigate the Social Costs of Adjustment (PAMSCAD), is a group of projects focused specifically on women. For various reasons,[11] this WID component of PAMSCAD has been delayed, but finally came on stream in mid-1991. A group of Amedzofe women was selected to benefit from a loan through this scheme to finance palm oil and other small-scale agricultural production. The loan is supposed to be repaid with minimal interest to provide a rolling fund to finance women's projects from other groups. Although PAMSCAD-WID schemes have been set up in several districts in Volta Region, there are none as yet (March 1993) in Ho District. The Amedzofe women are still waiting.

Although the Ghana Government is now well into its Economic Recovery Programme (in theory the stabilization phase has passed and the country is moving towards "adjustment with growth"), its actions seem to have affected the lives of most villagers only minimally. True, there are those villagers who have been "redeployed," but these are men (reflecting the greater likelihood for men to be employed in the formal sector). In comparison with the hardships, decline, and shortages of the 70s, life in the villages is, at least, resourced. Village stores stock basic medicines (and there is now the Health Post for treatment), there is a branch of FASCOM (a government-initiated agency supplying fertilizer, tools and pesticides for farmers) in the village and the small village market has regular supplies of smoked fish, canned milk, sugar, and other basic goods. In addition, there is now regular transport in and out of the village (provided by private operators) in spite of constant problems with the roads. But this, according to Amedzofe informants, is the *status quo ante*, this is more or less how things were in the late 60s, before the years of decline. For a contrast let us now look at the village of Antoakrom in the Amansie West District of Ashanti.

Antoakrom

Antoakrom is in the Amansie West District, about 12 miles southeast of the newly created district capital Manso Nkwanta. Like Amedzofe the effects of structural adjustment have been felt by some individuals, but for many life has remained largely unchanged. The population has always tried to meet the demands of an unstable economy and the policies of structural adjustment have only added another dimension to this pattern.

Government policy rarely touches the day-to-day lives of women in Antoakrom.

Antoakrom is situated on the junction of two roads which link it and the surrounding villages to the market and business centers of Bekwai (the former district capital) due east, and Kumasi to the north. Antoakrom is the central focus for surrounding villages because of its situation on these cross roads. Until 1988 Bekwai was the district administrative center, and Antoakrom came under its authority, but the administrative focus has now shifted to Manso Nkwanta. Since the colonial period Antoakrom has been a local center for the administration of health and agricultural services and has cocoa offices, a local schools inspectorate division, a maternity home and clinic, and several banks (to deal primarily with the financing of cocoa).

The economy of the village is largely based on agriculture, and even those who have other employment farm if they can. There is a long association with cocoa growing in the area although more recently oil palm and maize have become important cash crops. Other crops that are widely grown include plantain, cocoyam, yam, and cassava. Rice is also planted, introduced to the area by the stranger population,[12] although it is a crop that is grown solely by men.

Women have access to their own lineage land, and may farm in their own right as well as helping their husbands on their farms. If women are widowed they may have rights to long-term crops such as cocoa on their dead husbands' land, but single and divorced women farm their own lineage land. There is no clear division between particular crops that are grown by men and others that are grown by women, although a far greater number of men grow crops that have a high imput of labor and/or cash, such as cocoa, oil palm, or rice.[13] On the whole men also have much larger farms than women.

Everyone who can grows surplus for the needs of the household, and many women make a living both trading the produce they themselves grow and also selling for their husbands. There is a small daily food market in Antoakrom, but most produce is sold out of the village. There is a nearby wholesale market that operates two days a week, and a large daily market in Bekwai about 16 miles away. Women from Bekwai market visit Antoakrom and the wholesale market regularly to purchase foodstuffs to resell.

Although farming and trading foodstuffs provides some income for most women in Antoakrom, they find it hard to make an adequate living. Government initiatives to help all farmers are few and far between, but women in Antoakrom and the surrounding area are ignored by government policy in general and under the aims of ERP in particular. Under ERP the government has pledged its commitment to making Ghana self-sufficient in food crops, but they do not fully recognise women's role in production. The goverment needs to help women specifically in the cash cropping of food crops and in the sale of these crops if they are to make the country self-sufficient, but their policies have a male bias. An example of this is in the availability of the extension services in Antoakrom.

The extension services are a way of reaching rural people, and the government recognizes the need for advisory help for small-scale farmers, but the extension service is understaffed and the staff underpaid. In 1989 the agricultural extension officer in Antoakrom was too busy farming for himself to offer very much help to anyone else. Those to whom he gave assistance asked for help themselves and could afford to utilize the advice given: they had money to buy pesticides and fertilisers or to hire labor. None of the women interviewed in both 1988–89 and 1991 had received any help from him, although some of the more wealthy male farmers who planted oil palm and grew rice and maize sought his help. Unless women have access to this kind of help in the same way as men, their levels of productivity will continue to be lower than those of their male counterparts whose farms are bigger and whose access to labor is more sure.

One of the specific aims of the government under ERP has been to reorganize publicly owned agricultural enterprises. This has meant sacking many workers who were surplus to requirements. This policy had a direct effect in Antoakrom in 1987 as 210 staff at the local government cocoa plantation and cocoa offices were made redundant. Of the 210 redeployees, 77 were women. For all of these workers, and especially the women, this caused great hardship. In spite of the fact that many of these workers were also farmers, their monthly salary, however small, was a substantial part of their cash income. This money paid for clothing, school books, fees, and uniforms, and medical bills as well as non-farm-produced food. In 1988 the local Agricultural Development Bank manager in Antoakrom said that he rarely gave loans to women since they could not afford to repay them. The only women to whom he had ever granted loans were those who were government employees with a monthly salary. So the women who had been redeployed in Antoakrom had not only lost a major part of their monetary income but also their chance of securing a loan.

In 1991 interviews were conducted with some of those who had been made redundant in Antoakrom to see if their lives had changed as a result. One of the women interviewed is a typical example of what has happened to the redeployees. She had been a laborer on the cocoa plantation, and when she was laid off in 1987 she was given two years basic salary as redundancy money. She received two thirds (96,000 cedis)[14] later the same year, and one third (57,000 cedis) in 1988. Like many of the women who were redeployed she was forced into the informal sector and decided to start trading. She used the money she received to buy a few personal items including a bed, but spent most of it setting up a business selling cloth. This was making her a meagre living in 1991, but many of her customers bought on credit and did not pay what they owed. Her salary had been small, but it was regular and guaranteed. In 1990, two years after they had been made redundant, PAMSCAD offered redeployees in Antoakrom loans to help with farming, or to establish a small business. But after initial meetings were held the redeployees heard nothing else. The same woman voiced the opinions of many of the redeployees when she said, "We have heard nothing, I do not think the money will come, they [PAMSCAD officials] are just making fun of us."

Of the sample of women interviewed in Antoakrom in 1991, 91% had never heard of the government's adjustment program or PAMSCAD, and knew nothing about their agendas. Of the few who had heard something, their ideas about the nature of these programs were very vague. This is hardly surprising considering that most of the details concerning structural adjustment and the activities of PAMSCAD appear in the press and on television, two sources of information that do not reach the majority of Antoakrom's population (there is no electricity in the village, and there are no newspapers locally available). In any case, relying on newspapers and other forms of written communication for publicity discriminates against women: almost half of the women in the Antoakrom sample (47%) had no education and another 47% had some primary education. It is safe to say therefore that more than half of the Antoakrom women could not read English, the language in which most newspapers and government notices and documents are written. Many of the Antoakrom women (and men)[15] who had been made redundant from their government employment knew little or nothing of changes in government policy and just shrugged their shoulders in response to questions. The ones who were aware of the meetings PAMSCAD had attempted to organize did not relate them to any policy or plan on the part of the government and almost all were unaware of the nature of PAMSCAD's role in the adjustment program. In Antoakrom as in Amedzofe, PAMSCAD to those who had heard of it, was an organization that might offer some form of assistance at some time in the future, but was not to be relied upon as a source of help.

Comparison

It is obvious from the descriptive accounts of Amedzofe and Antoakrom that they are very different in setting, history, and outlook. Antoakrom is perhaps the more typical rural settlement in Southern Ghana in terms of heavy reliance on cash crops with men predominating in their producton. Amedzofe's history and ecology has meant a greater reliance on migrant labor with farming being primarily for subsistence, the exception being the fruit trade from the 1940s to the 1960s. We can compare their "structures" in terms of descriptive statistics and also compare these stastistics with statistics derived from surveys carried out in two villages in the same districts, but with different locations and histories: Sokode-Bagble (Ho District) and Nsiana

(Amansie West). Bagble is about seven miles from Ho on the plain along the main road between Accra and Ho and has no history of strong links with church or education. Nsiana is about two miles northwest of Antoakrom along an unmade track. Although the ecology is similar to that of Antoakrom the village has none of Antoakrom's bustle, being some distance from a main road/junction. Table 1 shows occupational profiles for both women and men in all four villages. The occupations assigned to people in the following tables are those claimed by respondents[16] as their main occupation in the villages. What is immediately apparent is that although, as we should expect, the most frequent rural occupation is farming, there is no "typical" pattern that emerges otherwise. The occupational profiles are dependent largely on location and history. Bagble has a high proportion of women traders, reflecting both the tradition of its women selling in local markets and its location so close to Ho (the regional capital) and on a relatively good road. Antoakrom, too, has a relatively high proportion of women traders, again reflecting its position at a junction and, historically, as a center for the coca trader. (A significant number of Antoakrom's women traders are in fact cooked-food sellers who supply the government workers and travellers through the village). Although only 16% of women present in Amedzofe said they were traders, 26% of all Amedzofe women in the sample were said to be traders (including migrants): Amedzofe, although remote, is a relatively large settlement and has a long history of its women working "away."

While Bagble's women are very active in trading, its men may well have trained in a craft specialization such as carpentry, bricklaying, or stone-masonry. Amedzofe's men, on the other hand, are those most likely to be in receipt of pensions from a formal sector job (26%).[18] The prevalence of these two occupational categories/sources-of-income among men in the Ho District accounts for the difference, between Ho District and Amansie West, in the proportions of men stating that their main occupation was farming.

Table 1.
Comparative proportion (%) of women and men in four
Ghanaian villages involved in selected occupations.

| | Ho District | | | | Amansie West | | | |
| | Amedzofe | | Bagble | | Antoakrom | | Nsiana | |
	W	M	W	M	W	M	W	M
Farmer (%)	55	45	45	50	62	71	75	74
Artisan (%)	0	9	6	24	0	7	4	3
Unemployed (%)	8	8	5	11	2	5	0	2
Trader (%)	16	2	37	2	24	5	6	2
Teacher (%)	12	5	4	3	3	14	12	12
Retired (%)	7	26	1	8	8	0	3	7
Totals	85	65	155	93	87	44	68	58

W= women M=men

When we look at the proportions of villagers who stated they
were teachers, then there are problems created by the relatively
small size of the sample. Although 12% of Nsiana sample
women were teachers, the actual number is 8, which is skewed
since one of the houses in the Nsiana sample was composed
almost entirely of (immigrant) teachers from the village school.
Perhaps a better indication of the relative proportions of teachers among our four populations can be gained from the figures
in the total sample, that is, including migrants (Table 2).

Table 2.
Proportion of teachers in total sample
(including migrants).

	Women	Men
Amedzofe	21	24
Bagble	8	8
Antoakrom	6	12
Nsiana	14	11

The Nsiana percentage for women is probably still disproportionately inflated, but the comparative figures from the other villages give an indication of a broader pattern. Because of its history, Amedzofe has had a relatively high proportion of both women and men going into teaching (which also helps to account for the larger number of pensioners in Amedzofe!). What is interesting here is that in each village the disparities in the proportions of men *vis a vis* women who have become teachers are quite small. Under the former education system, primary and middle school teaching was one escape route from farming for villagers. Teacher training at these levels was government funded and required only a middle school leaving certificate as entry qualification, and most villages, certainly in southern Ghana, either had a middle school or were near enough to allow village children to attend a school in a neighboring village.[19] With the government's education reforms, however, teacher training has been significantly reorganized and only those who have recognized *secondary* school leaving qualifications will be eligible to become teachers. On past evidence, this will discriminate heavily against women.

Table 3 is a comparison (among those people over 18 in each of the villages) of educational attainments by gender. Both those who have completed their education and those who are still undergoing some form of education are included so that an impression can be gained of the patterns of education in each village. In the Volta Region villages there is a greater emphasis on teacher and vocational training (nurses, agricultural workers). Only from Amedzofe, which has such a close historical association with education, is there anyone, whether male or female, who is currently training at the post-secondary level.

The numbers of women and men from the four villages currently in secondary school are small (women proportionately smaller in number than men), but perhaps the remarkable feature, in the light of changes in the educational system, is that so few are either in vocational or teacher training now. After junior secondary school (which has replaced the middle schools), students who go on are supposedly streamed either into new senior secondary schools, which offer academic education, or into technical schools, which offer accredited skill training. Whereas there doesn't appear to have been a tradition of teacher or vocational training in Amansie West in the past (and still not today), the level of taking up further training, either skill training or as teachers, in Ho District has dropped quite markedly. As we stated, only Amedzofe out of all of our 4 sites[20] has any students either currently in or who have already completed post-secondary teacher training, which has replaced, and is intended to upgrade primary and junior secondary teacher training.

Table 3.
Level of education by gender in four Ghanaian villages.

| | Ho District | | | | Amansie West | | | |
| | Amedzofe | | Bagble | | Antoakrom | | Nsiana | |
	W	M	W	M	W	M	W	M
None (%)	8	4	16	8	47	19	36	14
Up to middle (%)	59	42	69	64	47	62	57	65
Completed secondary or higher (%)	7	19	2	14	1	2	4	9
Teacher/vocational (%)	21	18	11	6	2	3	1	6
Current secondary or higher (%)	2	9	1	5	3	9	1	5
Current teacher/ vocational (%)	2	6	2	3	0	3	1	1
Current post secondary (%)	1	2	0	0	0	0	0	0
Total (n)	230	214	268	220	116	94	84	80

A major thrust of the government's adjustment policies is the orientation towards export agriculture, cash-cropping for export. A prime weapon in this campaign is the government-funded Agricultural Extension Service and its associated specialist branches such as the Cocoa Services Division. Both Amedzofe and Antoakrom had a resident field extension officer: in Antoakrom, as we have seen, he was preoccupied with his own concerns and in Amedzofe, although from the locality and therefore familiar with local mountain farming conditions (and the language), was not dynamic and was largely invisible in the life of the village. Table 3 shows the proportions of women and men in each village who had used the services of the field extension officer.

Table 4.
Proportions (%) of women and men consulting Agricultural Extension Services.

Location	Women		Men	
	Yes	No	Yes	No
Amedzofe (%)	43	57	49	51
Antoakrom (%)	0	100	50	40

In Antoakrom, in the heart of the Ashanti cocoa-growing area, no women had consulted the Agricultural Extension Services in spite of the endemic presence of cocoa diseases. This seems to accord with information from elsewhere in the cocoa-growing areas that indicates that women are increasingly more peripheral with respect to cocoa growing. Since Ghana's development strategy is largely focussed on the production of exports, and cocoa is a (if not the) major export crop, this failure in the consultation/advice process at the grassroots implies that women are being left out of the current drive for cocoa exports. Palm oil is the popular local alternative to cocoa as a cash crop and, as stated above, few women have the capital to begin oil palm farming. In Amedzofe, where cocoa is not such a significant source of income, then both women and men have at least consulted the local field officer, attempting to seek advice both for existing food crops and for diversifying into new cash crops.

However, if we look at the bases on which people had dealings with the Agricultural Extension Services, then we can see just how marginal the extension services, a long-term institution in Ghana, are to the rural people (Table 5).

The "practical" advice tended to be in the form of seeds and fertilizer in Amedzofe and of crop spraying in Antoakrom. The relatively large "other" category in Amedzofe was advice and help in connection with the potato-growing cooperative in the mid-1970s.

Table 5.

Relative proportions (%) of women and men in two villages who received help from Agricultural Extension Services.

	Women		Men	
	Amedzofe	Antoakrom	Amedzofe	Antoakrom
Advice	43	0	9	43
Practical	14	4*	21	7
Other	0	0	19	0
None	43	96	51	51

*One women said her farm had been sprayed, although she said she had not consulted the Agricultural Extension officer.

It would be all too easy to portray this essentially negative picture of the Agricultural Extension Services as the consequences of the poor state of the services in Ghana in spite of inputs and exhortations to produce for the export market. However, the image is belied by the Agricultural Extension experiences from Bagble. Here, the officer is a woman from Bagble itself and she has been very active in organizing loose cooperative groups to try to attract funding from organizations such as Global 2000. In addition, however, the Bagble villagers do tend to use fertilizers and plant their maize and cassava in rows and refer in conversations about their farms to the extension officer by name. The fact that both Amedzofe and Bagble are both in the same administrative district, are subject not only to the same policy but to the same relatively senior officers, and have such different experiences of and relations with their local officers reflects the caution that must be exercised in making overall generalizations: it depends on the local officer's personality, his/her relations with the community, at least as much as on what resources are available. The question of gender too might well be significant but at present it is only in Volta Region (where Ho District is) that there is even a small proportion of women extension officers. This is a situation that is planned to change within a few years as more female officers are trained.[21]

There is a great disparity between the proportions of women and of men who have ever received loans in both Amedzofe and Antoakrom. In Amedzofe none of the women in the sample had received a loan, while in Antoakrom 77% had never had a loan. The proportions of men in these villages who had never had a loan were 63% and 64%, respectively. But, as noted earlier, bank officials seem to be unwilling to give loans to women. Although men had loans through banks, the Antoakrom women's loans had come from the local *susu* organization,[22] that is, they were not formally negotiated loans, official in any fiscally conventional way. In addition, the questions we asked were about *ever* having loans, and many of those who had received loans had done so before the collapse of the economy in the mid- to late-70s. Loans under the present dispensation, although officially encouraged in the agricultural sector, have been scarce, the experiences of the Antoakrom villagers with the promises of PAMSCAD being typical.

Table 6.

Knowledge of the Economic Recovery Programme (ERP) and the Programme of Actions to Mitigate the Social Costs of Adjustment (PAMSCAD) by village and by gender.

| | Ho District | | | | Amansie West | | | |
| | Amedzofe | | Bagble | | Antoakrom | | Nsiana | |
	W	M	W	M	W	M	W	M
Heard of ERP (%)	43	49	4	25	9	39	0	16
Not heard of ERP (%)	57	51	96	75	91	61	100	84
Heard of PAMSCAD (%)	86	77	4	29	9	61	11	52
Not heard of PAMSCAD (%)	14	23	96	71	91	39	89	48

Finally, we turn to the villagers' knowledge of and interaction with the current government programs and plans. We asked generally whether people in the villages had heard of the Economic Recovery Programme (referred to as "ERP" by people who have heard about it[23]), and specifically whether they had heard of PAMSCAD which, above all, is supposed to be effective at the grassroots level. Table 6 shows the results of those questions.

Here again we can see a marked disparity among our survey sites in the knowledge of government policies and programs. There are no media differences among the sites: none have electricity on a regular basis and none receives regular deliveries of newspapers. Information comes to the villages through loca-language news bulletins on radios (battery operated!) and through visits and contacts with those working away, as well as through government agents such as extension officers, CDR officials, and those from the 31st December Women's Movement.[24] Amedzofe has more people working away (but is certainly much more difficult to get to than either Antoakrom or Bagble), but the key to the high level of claimed knowledge of ERP and PAMSCAD in Amedzofe is probably both the facts that the CDR officials and the chief and his elders are relatively well informed (and well integrated in the village) and that Amedzofe has been the recipient of PAMSCAD Community Development funding to build a latrine block. The block was "inaugurated" with great ceremony by visiting PAMSCAD officials less than six months before we began our work. Of those women in our Amedzofe sample, even so shortly after this grand opening ceremony, almost one third said that they knew the name only, not what it signified or what its purposes were; 43% said that it gave community help; and only 14% said that PAMSCAD "built latrines."

Amedzofe shows rather anomalous results in Table 6. In all of the other rural survey sites, male knowledge of government policies well outstrips female knowledge, which conforms to the generally held idea that women are more peripheral to the cash economy and to political life.[25] It may well be that the results from Amedzofe on spread of knowledge of PAMSCAD among women are an outcome of both the presence of a PAMSCAD-funded project in the village as well as an active 31st December group (and a relatively well-educated population). In addition, the positive information about agricultural extension from Bagble, where the extension officer is a local woman, suggests that at least a subset of "pictures from Ghana" may not be all doom and gloom. But at present the factors that appear to promote women's welfare in rural areas are particularistic: a particularly active and well-integrated branch of 31st December Women's Movement or an enthusiastic and well-informed female extension officer.

Although (the new) government rhetoric now insists that 31st December is *not* a party organ, it still is overwhelmingly connected with the agency of Nana Konadu Agyeman Rawlings, its founder, in the minds of most Ghanaian women, and the new government won only minority support in the Ashanti Region. 31st December Women's Movement still has an uphill struggle to become a widespread and effective grassroots women's community organization.[26] Similarly, in spite of great enthusiasm among the senior women extension officers in Ho for expanding the work of women as field officers and in spite of ostensible government commitment to training women officers, with the retrenchments in the Civil Service (of which Agricultural Extension forms a part) even the most avid women senior officers admit that the prospects for employing women as field officers on a nationwide basis are extremely long-term. Field officers who are leaving now are not being replaced because of lack of funds. Nsiana does not have a resident extension officer.

But these kinds of comments and views have been expressed in Ghana again and again during the past 30 years, and although we have made them with specific reference to women's organizations and agricultural extension, to women's income earning oppportunities and education, similar observations could be made on other areas of life. What we suggested in the introduction was that rural life in Ghana has not changed very much: its patterns of resourcing, its rewards, its difficulties, and its peaks and troughs. In effect: *"plus ca change, plus c"est la meme chose...."*

BIBLIOGRAPHY

Brydon, Lynne, 1976, *Status Ambiguity in Amedzofe-Avatime: Women and Men in a Changing Patrilineal Society,* Unpublished Ph.D. Thesis, University of Cambridge.

Brydon, Lynne, 1979, Women at Work: Some Changes in Family Structure in Amedzofe-Avatime, *Africa* 49 (2), 92 - 111.

Brydon, Lynne, 1985, The Avatime Family and Migration: 1900-1980, in *Circulation in Third World Countries*, (eds) Murray Chapman and Mansell Prothero, Routledge, 206 - 225.

Brydon, Lynne, 1992, Ghanaian women in the migration process, in *Gender and Migration in Developing Countries*, (ed) Sylvia Chant, Belhaven Press: 91 - 108.

Brydon, Lynne and Karen Legge, forthcoming, *Adjusting Ghanaian Society: Ghanaians, The World Bank and the IMF.*

Mikell, Gwendolyn, 1991, "Equity Issues in Ghana's Rural Development", in *Ghana: The Political Economy of Recovery*, (ed) Donald Rothchild, SAIS African Studies Library: Lynne Rienner, Boulder and London:85 -100.

NOTES

1. Brydon has worked in and around the Avatime area since 1973 and Legge has worked in Antoakrom since 1987.

2. A traditional area is the area overseen by a paramount chief: it is, effectively, the lowest unit of local government in Ghana.

3. L. Brydon, Status Ambiguity in the Amedsofe-Avatime: Women and Men in a Changing Patrilineal Society, Ph. D. diss. (unpublished), University of Cambridge, 1976; see also: L. Brydon, Ghanaian Women in the Migration Process, in S. Chant, ed., *Gender and Migration in Developing Countries* (Bellhaven Press, 1992) pp. 91–108.

4. L. Brydon, "Women at Work: Some Changes in Family Structure in Amedzofe-Avatime," *Africa* 49, 2 (1979): 92–111; see also: L. Brydon, "The Avatime Family and Migration: 1900–1980," in: Murray Chapman and Mansell Prothers, eds., *Circulation in Third World Countries* (City-??: Routledge, 1985), pp. 206–225.

5. The mean household sizes we found in our work were all considerably larger than those suggested by data from the Ghana Living Standards Survey, the 'official' Government/ World Bank survey designed to monitor the effects of adjustment. Disrepancies between the GLSS data and our own and problems with the GLSS methodology will be taken up in other publications.

6. There is very little opportunity either for women or men to work in formal sector manufacturing since there is so little of it in Ghana and what there is is concentrated on a few sites such as Tema. There were also no instances of out-working/ home-working in our samples.

7. As early as 1956, the geographer, H.P. White, noted the impending population pressure on land in the mountains around Amedzofe: he saw emigration as a response to growing population pressure.

8. One of the standard forms of contract allowed this.
9. In interviews carried out in 1974, Brydon asked what men and women did with the separate income they earned. The responses were almost uniform: if they had any sense, people said, they should use the money together to care for the children (Brydon, 1976:Chapter 5).
10. It is the chiefs and elders who are responsible for organising communal labour, usually the male chiefs and elders. In addition there has been a Town Development Committee (mostly, if not all, male) in existence since the 1960s but it was moribund. Since the de-politicisation of the Committees for the Defence of the Revolution, the personnel of the Amedzofe CDR (male) seem to have taken over the functions of the TDC.
11. L. Brydon and K. Legge, *Adjusting Ghanaian Society: Ghanaians, The World Bank and the IMF* (forthcoming).
12. The strangers are migrants from the north of Ghana who initially came to work in the gold fields and timber industry and who subsequently settled in Antoakrom to farm.
13. In 1988 only 5 women from a sample of 40 had oil palm farms, and none grew rice. In 1990 this figure had increased slightly with 3 other women from the 1988 sample cultivating oil palm.
14. The cedi is the unit of Ghanaian currency. In early 1993 there were about 340 cedis to one US dollar.
15. Nineteen percent of Antoakrom men had no education and 62% had up to Middle School leaving qualifications.
16. In each site at which we worked we interviewed in 50 households. There are basic demographic data on each members, present and absent of the sample households and also more detailed information on farms, crops grown (in rural areas) and occupation and family incomes (in urban areas), together with information on community participation and socioeconomic information pertaining to housestyle and ownership of consumer goods. More detailed information from our work will be available in our forthcoming book (Brydon and Legge, *Adjusting Ghanaian Society, op. cit.*).
17. Brydon and Legge "Avatime Family and Migration."
18. The relatively high proportion of women from Antoakrom (8%) in this category is, unfortunately, a product of coding. Those who were in receipt of pensions were coded together with those who were too old to farm anymore and relied on their families for support. No woman in the Antoakrom sample was in receipt of a pension.
19. The same is not true of northern Ghana. We carried out a survey among a very small sample (therefore not included in the main body of our analysis here) of households in a village in

the Northern Region. This village did not have a middle school, nor, at present does it have or has plans to build, a Junior Secondary School. It is not atypical of the North.

20. Scanning our data from 2 urban areas support these observations. There are no students from our urban samples (from Nima in Accra and from Tamale) currently in Post-Secondary teacher training.

21. Recent information (March, 1993) from Ghana suggests that there are also female agricultural workers taking part in a series of Canadian Government funded projects in the Northern Region.

22. *Susu* is an organisation to which a group of people contribute money on a regular basis. The total is available for loans to each member of the group in turn. It is based on the Yoruba *esusu*, 'rotating credit' organisation.

23. When we designed our set of questions, initially we had questions referring to 'structural adjustment', but we rapidly found that even fewer people in the villages knew that term than 'ERP'.

24. Space does not permit us to comment in detail upon the variations in effectiveness of these latter two organisations at the local level. In Amedzofe 31 December is very well organised and active, in Nsiana and Antoakrom, ineffective to the point of non-existence and in Bagble, split by factionalism which renders it ineffective. This gives a more textured version of the local tentacles of 31 December than the more usual blanket versions for example that given by Mikell (1991).

25. See, for example, Gwendolyn Mikell, "Equity Issues in Ghana's Rural Development," in: Donald Rothchild. ed., *Ghana: The Political Economy of Recovery* (Boulder/London: SAIS African Studies Library, 1991), PP. 85–100.

26. For a view from Brong Ahafo see Milkell, *op.cit.*

CHAPTER SEVEN

ENGENDERING THE ADJUSTMENT PROCESS IN TRINIDAD AND TOBAGO: PERSPECTIVES AND POLICY ISSUES

Gwendoline Williams and Ralph Henry[1]

INTRODUCTION

Since the Decade of Women which culminated in the World Conference in Nairobi, Kenya in 1985, there has been increasing concern, particularly in developing countries, over the need for a more gender-aware approach in shaping and implementing public policy. Gender, like the other social categories of class, race, age, and rural/urban differentiation, is a key determinant of the way in which policy programs impact upon the quality of life of a population. Hogwood and Gunn see public policy as a process that has several facets and stages of planning and action. In its earliest phase, public policy "expresses the broad purposes or 'ends' of government activity . . . and also describes the state of affairs which would prevail on the achievement of those purposes."[2] Following the statements of intent, specific proposals usually emerge. These are the formal authorization for programs and projects, the outcome of which is assessed in order to evaluate the effectiveness of public policy. Increasingly, among other factors, this effectiveness is measured by the extent to which explicit consideration is given to gender.

This perspective on public policy is a useful basis for the examination of gender-awareness in the period of severe economic decline of the economy of Trinidad and Tobago in the 1980s. Official documentation substantiates that the period under review, from 1982 to 1987, was one of negative economic performance. Petroleum sector earnings fell by close to 50%, unemployment increased to 22%, and real gross domestic product (GDP) for 1987 was 28% below the 1982 level. Reasons for this economic downturn include the collapse of oil prices, declining oil production, poor economic management during the oil boom, problems with diversification and failure to develop more flexible production strategies.[3]

Strategies for recovery proposed by the government included the adoption of stabilization and structural adjustment measures. An additional concern of the political leadership was that control measures should ensure "as much fairness and equity as is humanly possible in the adjustment process," including "some measure of protection for the weakest and most defenseless members of the society."

This developing concern in Trinidad and Tobago, with the need for adjustment, reflected regional anxieties dating back to the 1970s, about adverse changes in terms of trade, oil-price increases, external debt service, and declining productivity in key sectors of the economy.

The acceptance and adoption of the strategy of structural adjustment led to the reduction in subsidies on basic items of consumption, price increases in goods and services, import reduction, and the drastic re-allocation of manpower and other resources among sectors of the economy. The three-year Public Sector Investment Program (PSIP), unveiled in 1988, detailed projects to diversify the Energy Sector, promote tourism, manufacturing, and agriculture (to earn and, in the case of agriculture, save foreign exchange). The projects had implications for employment in the short run, but the hoped for impact was the creation of permanent jobs in viable enterprises targeted in the international market.

However, it is the purpose of this chapter to examine the impact of the erosion of the 1974/82 gains in health education, housing, and social development on significant social groups, including women and children.

ELEMENTS OF A GENDER-AWARE APPROACH

It is now widely acknowledged that gender with respect to the position of women in the development process has not been a significant variable in public policy studies and the analysis of macroeconomic or sectoral policies. This is a grave shortcoming insofar as it reflects the underutilization and inadequate recognition of a very significant proportion of the world's human resources. The 1980 Copenhagen statement pointed out the insidious effect of policy measures which result in half the world's population performing two-thirds of the world's work, receiving one-tenth of the world's income, and owning less than one per cent of the world's property.

In explaining this gross maldistribution of resources, Moser[4] identified two fundamental misrepresentations: firstly, the widespread tendency to assume that the male-headed household is the dominant type, with the man as the producer and his wife the reproducer; secondly, planners' blindness to the contributions of women in the wider economic, community, and political spheres.

The extensive role played by women in the economic, political, and social spheres as well as in household management needs to be recognized in policy statements, programs, and projects. Women must be seen both as contributors to and as beneficiaries of development. A recent report on gender issues in development made reference to the utility of a "gender lens" that should be used to modify existing methods of policy planning in order that the gender variable receive treatment at each phase of policy formulation and implementation. This approach is very different from that which views women as a special interest group and opens up the possibility of governments taking responsibility for considering gender when shaping public policy.

OBJECTIVES OF THE PRESENT STUDY

The objectives of our study are to examine from a gender-sensitive perspective the policy shifts following the adoption of the structural adjustment program in Trinidad and Tobago and to assess the impact of the program on the position of women. The non-explicit treatment of gender in the policy planning process has helped to create and maintain the "invisibility" of women as key contributors to and beneficiaries of public policy.

Labor Force Impact

In 1964, 23% of the labor force was employed in the sector of agriculture, forestry, hunting, and fishing. This sector was the second largest employer of women, who formed 31% of those employed (women outnumbered men in the service sectors). But in the 1970s this sector declined in importance and its share of the labor force fell to 13.1% by 1975, at which time women constituted 24% of the work-force employed in agriculture, forestry, hunting, and fishing. The sector continued in decline over the following ten years, at which point the fall in oil prices triggered a shift in employment patterns.

A major problem of oil-exporting countries has been their inability to transform their economies at exactly the point in time when financial resources are available for diversification and the reduction of dependence on oil revenue. This has been described as the OPEC varient of "Dutch Disease," so-called after Holland's famous experience of this problem of deindustrialization. In the case of Trinidad and Tobago, the "Dutch Disease" affected agriculture in particular, as domestic supplies became uncompetitive with imported food.[5] Moreover, employment in government work-relief programs, which carried higher effective wages than many other sectors, reduced the supply of manpower for the more demanding tasks in agriculture. Oil revenue allowed for massive government expenditure and created numerous inefficiencies in the economy, presaging the enormous difficulties that attended the inevitable decline in oil prices.[6]

Significant among these difficulties was the collapse in employment that was directly linked to government expenditure. Trinidad and Tobago proved to be no exception to countries with "Dutch Disease." As oil revenues plummeted there was an immediate cutback or postponement of government projects and a decrease even in the basic maintenance function. Registered unemployment of just under 10% in the early 1980s, which was a kind of "full employment unemployment" for Trinidad and Tobago at that time, was to rise and exceed 20% by 1987. Since there was relatively less retrenchment in the public sector than the private, its share in employment increased.

Agriculture, as the sector most capable of relying on domestic resources and generating output to satisfy domestic demand, showed constant growth in output. Its share of GDP rose from 0.3% to 4.7% between 1984 and 1988. Employment in agriculture turned upward but the incidence percentage of women employed in the sector continued to decline to about 18% by 1987. However, since men tend to be registered as own-account farmers, their wives' contributions to family income may be underrecorded or unrecorded particularly when the man is engaged in formal sector employment and his wife tends the farm. In addition, many rural women in the Indian community are engaged in home production for sale. This too is under-recorded, although there is visual evidence of increased activity in this area.

The increased participation of women in the construction industry, including electricity and water supply, is an interesting development. This industry, as in so many countries, was considered the natural preserve of men. In the 1960s a mere 4% to 6% of the labor force were women. The boom in the industry created a massive demand for labor, eroding some of the traditional barriers to the employment of women. Training opportunities were available for women in established state institutions. By 1981, women were 15% of the workforce in this sector. It is noteworthy, however, that women in the construction industry

Table 1.
Selected Labor force data for Trinidad and Tobago

	December 1964			December 1968			December 1975			December 1981		
	Labor Force	Percent Female	Percent Female unemployed[1]	Labor Force	Percent Female	Percent Female unemployed	Labor Force	Percent Female	Percent Female unemployed	Labor Force	Percent Female	Percent Female unemployed
Agriculture, forestry, hunting and fishing	77,300	31	5 (7)	73,200	29	4 (8)	50,500	24	6 (8)	35,700	29	7 (5)
Mining, quarrying, and manufacturing	64,800	19	18 (11)	61,900	24	16 (14)	75,700	20	11 (11)	74,700	24	9 (7)
Construction (including gas, electricity, and water)	36,600	4	37 (20)	52,700	6	38 (25)	60,000	11	45 (24)	109,700	15	38 (17)
Commerce	45,900	38	10 (9)	50,400	34	8 (8)	67,300	42	9 (6)	78,500	52	6 (5)
Transportation and communication	24,100	7	15v (10)	24,600	7	14 (10)	28,900	8	4 (7)	33,800	12	14 (7)
Services	73,300	56	16 (12)	86,800	59	15 (12)	85,500	41	10 (8)	95,800	46	9 (6)
Never worked	11,800	54		10,600	55		15,100	56		7,000	67	
Labor force[2]	333,900	31	18 (14)	360,900	32	17 (15)	386,100	28	19 (15)	438,700	34	15 (10)

1. Figures in parentheses ae national unemployment rates for the sector.
2. Includes "not stated."
Source: Henry R. M. Jobs, Gender and Development Strategy in the Commonwealth Caribbean in Mohamed P.and Shepherd C. Gender in Caribbean Development Women and Development Studies Project, The University of the West Indies, St. Augustinee, 1988.

continued to have higher unemployment rates than men. In 1981, the unemployment rate for women in the industry was 38% as compared with a national average of 17% for the industry. By the end of 1987, some 73% of women in the industry were unemployed as compared with the overall rate of 46%.

The correlate of the decline in jobs at established firms was a growth in self-employment in those sectors where it was practicable. In this regard, it is useful to examine the growth of commerce and services between 1964 and 1981. Employment in these sectors grew by 58% and 31% respectively, over the period, as compared with growth of almost 200% in the construction sector. This growth reflected an increase in consumer demand in the distributive trades, retailing, and personal and community services. That employment in these sectors continued to grow after the economic downturn had less to do with real generation of jobs and more with changes in the employment market, as self-employment and shared employment replaced more productive jobs. From 1982, Trinidad and Tobago witnessed a massive increase in informal sector activities, with large numbers of people entering the small-scale retailing trade which characterizes many other Third World countries: hawking newspapers, lottery tickets, and other forms of street vending.

The relative dominance of women in commerce and services reflects women workers' search for relief from unemployment by engaging in job-sharing in sectors where ease of entry offers the opportunity of eking out a living with long hours and low rates of pay. There was a fall in the contribution of commerce and services to GDP between 1984 and 1988, which underlines the fact that the increase in employment, particularly of women, during this period was accompanied by falling output and reduced earnings. Since one-third of women employed in this sector would have been single heads of households, this drop in earnings created a crisis situation for them.

Manufacturing, quarrying, and mining also underwent a decline in employment. But, given the general absence of women from the latter two sectors, the effect of the downward trend on women is almost entirely located in the manufacturing sector. This sector was built on an import-substitution regime with a high level of protection, which rendered it incapable of competing on export markets when domestic demand collapsed. The garment and light-assembly industries are examples of sectors from which women workers were forced out and gravitated to commerce and services. Over the years, there has been a consistent tendency for unemployment among women to exceed the overall unemployment rate.

There was a substantial improvement in public sector participation of women between 1965 and 1973, as in the overall size of the workforce. While only 15% of women employed in the labor market were located in the public sector in 1965, by 1973 this incidence had risen to 26%. It continued to rise until 1987, when women were 35.2% in this sector. This illustrates the tendency towards parity of women in government as compared with in the total job market. Universalistic criteria are far more significant in the public sector than in the private and mobility has been easier for women.

The data do, however, mask the fact that women tend to be concentrated in certain fields and relatively absent from others: nursing, teaching, and clerical work are heavily biased towards women, who dominate the lower and middle levels. Their entry into the executive and management class in both the private and public sectors has been stymied. With the imminence of cutbacks in the public service sector as part of the stabilization and adjustment program, the clerical establishment is likely to be more seriously affected, with obvious implications for the employment of women.

Age-specific laborforce participation rates have been relatively stable across the labor force since 1965, but among women there has been a decline in participation in the 15- to 19-year-old age group, probably as a result of the expansion in public education facilities. The increase in the participation rates of women between the ages of 20 and 44 during the 1970s and early 1980s would have been attributable, in the main, to the buoyant economy and easy availability of jobs, but also to the increasing desire of women to put to use the improved education and training to which they had access.

However, the further increase in the participation rates of this group, together with the 45- to 54-year-old age group, concurrently with a decline in overall workforce participation, suggests that there has been an element of "added-worker" effect among women between the ages of 20 and 54 and is probably due to modernization and the increasing independence of women. Thus, as their menfolk become unemployed or experience the "discouraged worker effect," women seek out jobs or engage in self-employment in order to maintain a flow of income to the household. Obviously, in single female-headed households, the women have little choice.

Educational Provision

The 1980 Census revealed that approximately 28.7% of those employed were women. It also showed that while women were fairly well represented in the professional, technical, administrative, clerical, and sales categories of jobs, they were underrepresented in manufacturing, construction, transport, and agriculture. It is important to note that the growing equality of opportunity for education and training did not fully eliminate disparities in access to jobs and remuneration in the boom years of 1974-1982. These disparities will become more pronounced as the state and communities find it increasingly difficult to continue with affirmative action programs for recruitment, selection, and placement, particularly in the public sector.

Since certain sectors are still seen as the preserve of men, women are going to be forced into a highly bifurcated system of labor force participation. Either they qualify for high-level occupations in the professional, technical, administrative, and managerial streams, or they are reduced to the residual category of low level informal sector activities or to very specific female-oriented manufacturing as may take place in the export-processing zones, where low wages and unskilled labor will predominate. The apparent relative dominance of women in the higher levels may have something to do with constraints on their access to jobs seen as the preserve of men. Adjustment measures may further constrain such access, exacerbating inequitable labor market tendencies.

While it is true to say that women are reasonably well represented in professional, administrative/managerial, and clerical categories, distribution within these categories is interesting. While only 5.5% of those employed in architecture, engineering, and related areas were women, in medicine, dentistry and veterinary science women constituted nearly 70%. In other professional, technical, and related areas, the distribution of men and women was more or less even, but in the administrative and managerial group only 843 women were employed out of a total of 5,924 posts. Employment opportunities in manufacturing, construction, and transport were also scarce, and even in agriculture and related areas, the proportion of women was low. Career opportunity can be measured by the following:

- Provision for identifying individual areas of talent and skill
- Access to education and training, particularly at the secondary and tertiary levels
- Appropriate curriculum channels, unfettered by considerations of gender, class, race, or age
- Equity in job availability and placement
- Remuneration and career path progress on the basis of merit

The female university-student populations in Trinidad and Tobago increased appreciably between 1964 and 1976. Between 1980 and 1983 there were still more male registrants, but the difference continued to narrow. There were many more men in medicine and engineering, where the gap was widest, though there too it had begun to narrow. In the natural sciences the percentage of women students rose from 29.7% in 1980 to 41.9 in 1982. In law, agriculture, and social sciences there was a slight rise in the percentage of women students.

Career opportunities for graduates from eight randomly selected senior comprehensive schools in 1982 were examined for the National Training Board.[7] Some of the major findings were as follows:

A. While vocational graduates were more likely to find employment than nonvocational, vocational male graduates were more likely to find jobs than their female counterparts; this was the case in every job sector.

B. Vocational male graduates took a shorter time to find jobs

and were five times as likely to be self-employed, while female graduates had an unemployment rate of 55%.
C. In their first job, 51.9% of males and 40% of females found work related to their training.

Table 2.
Persons employed in a given week by
sex and occupation group

	Male		Female	
	No.	%	No.	%
All occupations	247,277	(100.00)	98,624	(100.00)
Professinal, technical and related architects, engineers, and related technicians	5,757	(2.33)	336	(0.34)
Medical, dental, veterinary, and related	1,714	(0.69)	3,750	(3.80)
Other professional, technical, and related	12,308	(4.98)	12,518	(12.69)
Administrative and mangerial	5,081	(2.05)	843	(0.85)
Clerical and related	20,402	(8.25)	29,031	(29.44)
Sales workers	15,332	(6.20)	12,071	(12.24)
Service workers	21,783	(8.81)	18,568	(18.83)
Agriculture, animal husbandry, forestry, fishermen, and hunters	24,058	(9.73)	4,496	(4.56)
Crafts and tradesmen	17,059	(6.90)	6,145	(6.23)
Construction workers	22,445	(9.08)	153	(0.16)
Transportation and equipment workers, including laborers	18,100	(7.32)	147	(0.15)
Other production and related workers, including laborers	78,840	(31.88)	9,075	(9.20)
Not stated, not elsewhere classified	4,398	(1.78)	1,491	(1.51)

Source: Central Statistical Office, Census of Population, 1980.

The study showed conclusively that there was no evidence that males were better trained than females, yet qualification requirements were more rigidly applied and wage rates significantly lower for women.

For the comprehensive female, curricula cannot override gender: their position in the labor market is in a sense pre-destined. This is, of course, irrational and totally unde-sirable, but a sobering reminder that tradition and preferences of employers (in the private sector at least) have a lot more to do with the way jobs are given out than any contrivance of the school.[8]

This pattern of disadvantage in the field of employment opportunities and remuneration can be expected to persist strongly under the conditions of adjustment accepted by the government.

Domestic Household Management

The economic downturn will continue to have a differential impact across households, not simply because of different economic circumstances but because of different household structures. While the index of average weekly earnings rose by 9.1% between 1985 and 1988, the cost of living rose by 28.5%, occasioning a substantial fall in real incomes of those employed in the formal sector.

Like other Caribbean countries, Trinidad and Tobago experienced slavery and indentureship and display a rich variety of family structures. Moreover, the Indian community, slightly larger than the African population at the last census, retains some characteristics of traditional forms of family organization brought by indentured laborers from India in the last century. Three major types of marital unions have been identified:
* Legal marriage with man and wife living together
* Common law unions where man and woman cohabit without a formal contract
* Visiting unions where a sexual relationship exists between man and woman but they do not live in the same household

Type of union is an indicator of economic managment in the household. Indian women have tended to enter their first, predominantly legal, union at an earlier age, to be part of extended households, and to have a higher average fertility than Afro-Trinidadian women. The latter tend to establish visiting unions, with a woman and her children forming the nuclear unit. Where an extended family unit does exist it is matrifocal.

The female-headed household, a phenomenon specific to the Afro-Caribbean community, is of special concern. Loss of a job imposes extra strain since the woman is the sole dependable breadwinner and generally lacks extended family support. With women experiencing higher unemployment rates than men and more likely to be relegated to sectors where employment sharing is the norm, these households are at particular risk.

The impact of the adjustment process on women can be assessed not only by the effect on women directly, but also on children, who, within all sub-groups, are in the care of their mothers. Thus, data on babies and young children serve as a good indicator of the quality of life of their mothers.

A feature of the recent period has been a rise in teenage pregnancies. While over the period 1955 to 1975, there was a decline in the specific fertility rate of the 15- to 19-year-old age group, from 181 per 1,000 to 82 per 1,000 females; thereafter it showed an upward movement, reaching 91 per 1000 in 1981.[9] From hospital records at five hospitals in 1987, it was calculated that 17% of births were to teenage mothers. The number of live births under 250g reached 13.5% of all births in 1987.[9] Protein-energy malnutrition affected 6% of children under age five in 1987, and was three times as likely to be found among low birth-weight children which in turn was associated with teenage pregnancy.[10] A high degree of acceptance and encouragement of early pregnancy was found in Tobago in 1986, and 76% of teenage mothers were still living with their parents.[11]

This increase in teenage pregnancies, together with the declining job market, particularly for females, surely exposes many teenage mothers and their children to poverty. The reduced importance of the extended family has not led to the development of adequate alternative support institutions. Only middle-income households can afford to employ help to supervise preschool children. A network of community-based day-care centers is being developed, but is by no means universal or of an adequate standard. Few such centers are situated near industrial estates or major concentrations of workers. So women using this service have to travel long distances, often at considerable expense because of the decline in public transport. Coverage of the nursery school system is also inadequate and the absence of or reduction in a school-feeding program contributed to a decline in enrollment in some areas.

A problem for women, almost specific to the Afro-Caribbean household, is the care of infirm parents, mostly mothers. Just as children are regarded as being the responsibility of their mothers, so do elderly parents tend to reside with daughters rather than sons. This puts excessive strain on the female household head particularly, since old-age or non-contributory pensions generally have not kept pace with inflation. No supporting infrastructure exists to help lower-income women who have to combine care for the aged with employment. Homes for the aged are few and mostly run by voluntary organizations with little financial support from the government.

Indigent households can apply for social assistance, but the criteria are exacting and it is usually given to adult males under retirement age only if they are incapacitated. Women and their children qualify if they can prove desertion by the husband or partner and can establish that they had tried unsuccessfully to have the court impose a maintenance order on the father of their children.

COMPARATIVE INFERENCES

Lack of gender-sensitivity in economic policies is not unrelated to failure to accord equity generally in development policy. For a brief period in the 1970s, especially after the promotion of basic needs strategies by the International Labor Organization, development literature argued for marrying equity and growth. However, persistent economic difficulties and failure to achieve growth soon directed the focus away from equity. The current wisdom, implicit in structural adjustment measures, is "grow now, redistribute later." Hence it is not surprising that gender equity comes even lower on the scale of priorities. The experience of stabilization under the International Monetary Fund has been extensive enough for its impact to be understood and analyzed. The verdict seems to be that, while economic measures may jolt an economy out of a stagnant mode, the social costs, which have been largely ignored, are significant and may fetter a society's development far into the future. Falling nutritional standards associated with the removal of subsidies on basic foods could have a deleterious effect for several generations on the quality of the workforce.

Equity can no longer be dismissed or postponed. If gender equity is to be achieved, there must be policies that ensure the continuing reduction in barriers to women's advance.

Training

Even when the economy declines, or when structural adjustment measures lead to drastic shifts in the pattern of output, training resources should be so distributed that women have an equal opportunity to be trained in sectors from which they have been traditionally excluded. There will be costs, such as the provision of child-care facilities. This principle should also apply to the reabsorption of teenagers in school when early pregnancy requires temporary withdrawal.

One critical area in which training is needed is with respect to the informal sector. Business-development courses must enable women to combine childbearing and childrearing with attendance and, ultimately, with labor-force participation. Needs such as time-management, budgeting, and skills upgrading must be addressed by training institutions.

Business Development Support

There is need for appropriate institutional support for small-scale activity, by way of credit (since lower-income women usually lack collateral), links with development agencies, and the creation of mechanisms to enable women and men to subcontract to larger enterprises in the formal sector.

Social Policy

A range of areas needs to be addressed to ensure that structural adjustment measures are more benign in their impact on women, and are gender-sensitive. These should include day-care facilities for the young and old in all housing development. Family Life Education is now on the school curriculum. The wider public also should be addressed, to sensitize men and women to the problems of household managment, particularly in times of economic stress. This should include shared decision-making, financial management, and birth planning. Failure to establish appropriate mechanisms has resulted in domestic destabilization and brought a host of problems for women. The level of social assistance and its expansion must be addressed because of the increase in unemployment. In the short term, policies should be directed at reducing the bureaucratic and legal hurdles faced by women in seeking assistance for their families.

An Inter-Sectoral Approach

Present public policy emphasis on fiscal and monetary considerations must be modified and a more interdisciplinary approach must be adopted that seeks to reconcile economic policy with social policy and political development. The state must adopt an interdisciplinary approach in negotiations with international lending agencies so that conditionalities of loan agreements are social-policy oriented. In view of the centrality of women in household managment, formal economic indicators must be augmented by indicators of household and community well-being. In other words, the success of stabilization and adjustment programs must be adjudged equally on the bases of economic *and* socioeconomic indicators.

The underlying principle should be that equity, including gender equity, is socially desirable and should have equal consideration with efficiency criteria in structural adjustment programs. In ignoring these issues a society runs the risk of undermining its longer term development, and thus its future economic efficiency. Gender equity should not be seen as pandering to women but as the sine qua non for the maintenance of human capacities and the quality of the whole population. Whether or not the economy is improving, policies must be directed at increasing equity generally, and that between the sexes specifically. Such measures should apply whether or not a country has embraced a structural adjustment program; however, their importance is heightened where a severe economic downturn has set it.

NOTES

1. A much longer paper on an allied theme has been published in S. Ryan, ed. *Social and Occupational Stratification in Contemproary Trinidad and Tobago*. Multimedia Production Centre, Faculty of Education, UWI, St. Augustine, Republic of Trinidad and Tobago, 1991.
2. Brian W. Hogwood, and Lewis A. Gunn, *Policy Analysis for the Real World* Oxford University Press, 1984.
3. Ministry of Finance and Economy, *Draft Medium Term Program, 1989-1991*, (Port of Spain: Government Printery, 1988).
4. Caroline O.N. Moser, *Housing Policy and Women: Towards a Gender Aware Approach* (mimeo), Development Planning Unit Workshop Paper No. 7, University College, London, 1985.
5. H. J. Pollard The Erosion of Agriculture in an Oil Economy: The Case of Export Crop Production in Trinidad, *World Development* 13, no. 7 (1985).
6. R. Auty and A. Gelb, Oil Windfalls in a Small Parliamentery Democracy: Impact on Trinidad and Tobago, *World Development* 16, no. 9 (1986).
7. India S. Harry, *Women In Agriculture in Trinidad,* unpublished M. Sc. thesis, University of Calgary, Alberta, Canada, 1980.
8. Theodore Lewis, *Labor Market Outcome of Comprehensive Education in Trinidad* (mimeo), National Training Board, Port of Spain, 1985.
9. Cynthia J. Rennie, Prevention of Childhood Malnutrition Through Interaction in the At-risk Adolescent in Trinidad and Tobago. *Caribbean Food and Nutrition Institute Quarterly,* Vol. 21.3. 1988.
10. C.E. McIntosh and J.A. Francis, *Report of the Sub-Committee on Health and Nutrition to Task Force on Food and Nutrition policy Formulation* (St. Augustine: Caribbean Food and Nutrition Institute, 1988).
11. N. Jack et al. *A Study in Teenage Pregnancy in Tobago* (mimeo), International Planned Parenthood Assoc. Antiqua, 1986.

CHAPTER EIGHT

GUYANESE WOMEN IN ACTION: RESPONSE AND REACTIONS TO ECONOMIC REFORM

Adeline Apena

This study addresses the responses and reactions of women to the challenge and impact of the Economic Recovery Program (ERP) in Guyana.

Our focus is not on the technical details of the program, but rather on how Guyanese women have been adjusting to and coping with the challenges, strains, and stresses unleashed by the program. We seek to explain what actions and activities women have undertaken to meet socio-economic realities of the situation either created or aggravated by the economic recovery measures. We examine the significance of such activities for the welfare of women and family in particular and of society in general.

In addition, we seek to demonstrate which of the measures undertaken by women are either traditionally female or non-female actions and activities. If we are able to show that women have gone beyond the sectors traditionally associated with women, then it may be possible to claim that the economic recovery measures have served as an impetus to women's actions. Finally, we would explain limitations to women's activities and the prospects for the future.

We make the following assumptions:

1. That the Economic Recovery Program was adopted at a period when the Guyanese economy was in a state of bankruptcy and paralysis
2. That the situation created a serious internal socioeconomic crisis in Guyanese history
3. That there was a downgrading of social services especially in health, education, and general infrastructure and essential facilities (water and electrical supply)
4. That in the short term, the economic recovery measures created conditions that seem to have aggravated the crisis
5. That women are the most severely affected by the impact of the measures because increasingly women are becoming heads of the households
6. That before the program women had been playing socioeconomic roles but that since the initiation of the measures women have increased their activities and are increasingly venturing into new areas beyond the traditional scope for women
7. That women have made serious inroads into self-employed activities
8. That there is an increase in the number of female associations
9. That these associations are empowering and facilitating women's actions and activities

INTRODUCTION

Guyana is located on the northern coast of South America. It is bordered by the Atlantic Ocean to the North, Venezuela to the West, Brazil to the South, and Surinam to the East. The only English-speaking state in South America, Guyana shares the same historical experience with the Caribbean Islands. Thus while history makes Guyana part of the Caribbean community, geography makes it South American. Guyana, the land of many waters, has 83,000 square miles of South American coast along the Atlantic.[1] The land area is as large as Britain and larger that the rest of the English-speaking Caribbean. But its population is barely 700,000.[2]

The interior, described as the "bush" by the Guyanese, consists of thick rain forests, vast savannah, mountains, and exotic waterfalls. More than 80% of this area is inaccessible, though it is rich in such minerals as gold, diamond, and manganese. The "bush" is sparsely populated. It holds only 3% of the total population. The coastal area constitutes 4% of the total land area, but contains more than 90% of the population. This represents a serious demographic imbalance. This factor has contributed to a disarticulate pattern of growth and development in Guyana.

Guyana is considerably diversified. There is diversity in race/ethnicity, religion, and cultural values, and, to a large extent, in political interests and inclinations. In terms of racial-ethnic compositions, African Guyanese (Guyanese of African decent) constitute 43% of the population, Indo-Guyanese (Guyanese of East-Indian origin) 51%, Amerindians (indigenous population) 4%, and others, including Portuguese, Chinese, and English, 2%.[3] With regards to religion, Christians constitute 55%, Hindu 36%, and Muslims 9%.[4] Politically, Guyana seems divided into political groups ranging from conservatives through moderate evolutionists to radical socialists.

These divisions have had serious consequences for the history of the Guyanese people and society. To a large extent the dissimilarities have created tensions in race relations as well as political conflicts and distrust. However it is difficult to ignore the psychological feelings of the different Guyanese groups who make claims to one nation with a common destiny.

ADOPTION OF ECONOMIC RECOVERY MEASURES

The story of the Economic Recovery Program dates to the first decade of political independence. The details of the causation of the program are the immediate concern of this paper. There are various explanations of the cause of economic decline and the consequent adoption of the reform measures. But there is a consensus among Guyanese that postindependence political actions and governance did not help to bring improvements to the economy. It is claimed that, at least, government actions failed to prevent or mitigate the steady decline of the economy.

Like most other Third World economies, the Guyanese economy relies on the production and export of raw materials for foreign exchange earnings. Guyana's export economy is based largely on bauxite, rice, and sugar. Economic decline implied that increasingly there were insufficient earnings from the export of these products. The story of decline in earnings has to do, in part, with fluctuations and depression in prices of these products in the international marked. In most cases, this factor did not encourage high-level productivity.

The bauxite industry was, according to Guyanese chairman Dunstan Barrow, in a precarious position. Only 65,000 tons of aluminum had been exported in 1982, compared to 165,000 the previous year. Rice production was 32,000 tons below target. Sugar production was close to its target but the industry continued to operate at a loss and is expected to do so for another two years.[5]

Consequently, the foreign reserves sank to less than $175 million in 1979. At the same time, the national debt was increasing. It rose $73 milion in 1979 and $1,800 billion in 1983. Table 1 shows details of the external debt.[6]

By the end of 1981, the economy had come to a halt and the nation was facing bankruptcy, It began to rank among the poorest of the Caribbean countries after Haiti. The $560 annual per capita gross national product of Guyana ranks the country among the poorest of Latin America and the Caribbean. More than 50% of the Guyanese people live in conditions of poverty, with extremely low income and high unemployment.[7]

The collapse of the economy was accompanied by massive deterioration in public services. Electric and water supply became inadequate. The sewage system and similar public services almost completely collapsed. Both the educational and health sectors were hard hit. Shortages of teachers, of basic textbooks, and of necessary equipment had severe adverse consequences on the school system.

The crisis was aggravated by the growing shortage of basic food items. Prices became inflationary. The black market grew rapidly. Businesses began to decline and collapse. Unemployment and underemployment became rampant. Social unrest and discontent were demonstrated in workers' strikes. The crisis was marked by a high rate of emigration. As people moved out, conditions deteriorated. Acute shortage of teachers and lack of basic textbooks and other essential materials gave Guyana the lowest level of education and school performance in the entire Caribbean. Similarly, shortage of water supply and deterioration in the sewage system seem to have increased mosquito breeding. The consequence is high incidence of ill health and disease. The health services declined rapidly from shortages of drugs, basic facilities, and medical personnel. One interviewee asserted:

> I don't know if the people went to the Georgetown hospital to get well or not. The place is such a misery. It is better not to face it. The conditions are too bad, they make a patient's condition worse. Imagine the mosquitos.[8]

On emigration:

> We that remain in Guyana are those that have no one to sponsor us, to help us get out of Guyana. We cannot afford a flight, have no one abroad to send us the cost of a ticket. I am ready to go anywhere to earn a better living standard. You know it is difficult to cope with the salary we get. Cost of things go up every day.[9]

It was these harsh realities that compelled the government to accept the conditions of the International Monetary Fund (IMF) in 1984 after negotiations to restructure the economy.

The IMF conditions were envisaged to provide answers to the economic problems and difficulties through a program of restructuring. Restructuring would enable the economy to recover from its paralysis. It was expected to get the economy in a more "realistic path."

Internationally, the IMF prescriptions are considered as measures meant to force a march towards a process of continuing growth, diversifications, and the strengthening of the economy in the long-run. They aim at sustaining economic growth and development through a process of structural transformation.[10]

In theory the measures are meant to ensure agricultural transformation and rural development, and to increase the degree of self-sufficiency in local food production. On closer examination, however, these objectives appeared to be in conflict with some of its prescriptions. The prescriptions emphasize development of new sources of foreign exchange earnings.

Seeking and developing new sources of foreign exchange earnings implies concentration on export-oriented production. This may mean less emphasis on nonexport production including food production. Reduction of cost of government operations means cutback in social services, layoffs, removal of subsidies, and price-control over food, health, and education. Also, continuing devaluation of the Guyanese dollar and liberalization of imports does not necessarily promote strong internal dynamics for ensuring economic growth and development. Implementation of Economic Recovery Measures in the short term aggravated economic difficulties. By far, women are the hardest hit. Women in Guyana have increasingly become managers of homes and households. Therefore they bear the brunt of more than 50% of the financial burdens of running households.

The policies affected women in three major ways:
1. Cutbacks in government expenditures have led to layoffs in public services. Women are more affected by this measure.
2. Removal of subsidies increased prices. Inflation is made worse by devaluation and growing black market conditions.
3. Government shifted emphasis from social services to debt servicing. Reduction of expenditures on social services increased cost of medicare, education, and other essential services. Women face the high cost of living, decline in real earnings, and have to cope with the increasing gap between real earnings and expenditures. A primary school teacher claimed:

I face increasing poverty. Prices go up every day. The salary is really small, it does not meet the cost of basic living. The rents are going up. It is hell. Except you know or have somebody overseas who can send you the dollar or pound, it is difficult.[11]

Women constitute more than 50% of Guyana's population. More than 50% of the rural population is female. Seventy percent of all women live in rural communities both in the interior (bush) and the coastal area.[12]

As already noted, women have increasingly become bearers of financial responsibility for households. This is due largely to the fact that more men have been emigrating and leaving the women in charge of the family. This is a moral issue which is not discussed in this work.

By the 1980–81 population census, women represent 25% of the labor force: 63% of the female population consider themselves housewives engaged in domestic duties.[13] However, this figure tends to underestimate the true participation rate of women in the work force. Women engaged in subsistence agriculture and other economic activities merely describe themselves as housewives rather than as farmers or other producers. Whether engaged in formal labor, in the informal sector, or unemployed, Guyanese women in general encounter social and economic difficulties.

WOMEN'S ASSOCIATIONS

This study focuses on women's associations as empowerment mechanisms for women's activities and reactions to the economic recovery measures. In this capacity, they fulfill the serious functions of sensitizing women to their potentials, and providing training in new skills, while improving old ones.

It may be claimed that not only do women's associations empower by strategizing for them but also they motivate and facilitate women's actions. In addition, they broaden opportunities for women through creating new outlets for application of skills. The number of women's associations increased during this period in response to the diverse and urgent needs of women. It is important to note that since 1975 the United Nations women's programs worldwide have promoted the formation of women's associations and energized women's activities.

This section examines the impact on women's activities made by three distinct women's associations — *The Mother's Union*, a Christian women's association; *CASWIG* (Conference on the Affairs and Status of Women In Guyana), an umbrella organization or non-governmental women's association, and *Red Thread*, a nonpartisan independent women's association.[14]

The Mother's Union

This association is the largest women's group within the Anglican communion worldwide.[15] It was founded by Mary Summer in England in 1876 and steadily spread to all parts of the British Empire. It has three goals:[16]
1. To uphold security and sanctity of marriage
2. To awaken in all mothers a sense of responsibility for their boys and girls as fathers and mothers of the future
3. To organize in every place a band of mothers who will unite in prayer and seek by their own examples to lead their families in purity and holiness in life.

Thus the Mother's Union was established to promote the welfare of families and of society. Our study concludes that this organization is oriented towards stabilization, improvement, and sustenance of society.

The Guyanese chapter of the Mother's Union was established in 1926 at All Saints Church, New Amsterdam in Berbice. It grew steadily from 43 branches in 1969 to 62 in 1991 with more than 1,100 members.[17] The scope of the association covers the entire country from the coast to the interior regions of Mazruni and Rupununi. Its expansion coincided with the growth of the Anglican church as a leading church in Guyana.

Since its establishment in Guyana, the Union has been involved in assisting women. Like other associations, its activities gained momentum since 1975. Its activities among the native Amerindian women have been considerably serious. To these rural women, the union represents a force of liberation and modernization. The actions of the union are in three main dimensions: general education and enlightenment campaign, promotion of skills through training, and provision of support services.

Education/Enlightenment

The union provides general education and public enlightenment on issues ranging from health, health-care, sanitation, and nutrition, to proper management of resources. This service is provided through regular seminars, workshops, and lectures. A minimum of six sessions is undertaken annually. The sessions serve as "eyeopeners" in the attempt to eradicate ignorance.

Skill Promotion

Training sessions are provided by the union to enable women to obtain new skills or improve old ones. This is largely in food-production and food-processing. Also new methods of production in art, crafts, and wine are taught. There is an emphasis on utilization of local resources in production. A total of twenty training sessions in various aspects were undertaken between 1985 and 1991. The significance of these actions is the acquisition of skills that enable and facilitate income generation. In addition, the programs provide opportunity for acquiring skills and therefore a source of livelihood for women. It may be noted that the majority of the skills encouraged are geared towards self-employment. Ultimately, these strategies stimulate entrepreneurial growth among women. Twenty-five Amerindian women participated in the 1991 Guyanese Women's Craft Fair. The union organizes outlets for marketing of their wares in the capital city of Georgetown. This promotes improvement of the earnings of rural women.

Reference has been made to shortage or lack of basic facilities in general. This situation is worse in Northern Guyana, which seems to have been sealed off from developments occurring in other parts of Guyana.

The union sponsored a water project in interior regions of Rupununi. The project was funded partly by the Pan-American Health Organization (PAHO). Bullock carts were also provided in the same region to facilitate movement of people and goods.18 Public transportation was paralyzed before 1985, and even when it had functioned it did not extend to the interior. Consequently, the area remained inaccessible. Communication within Rupununi and between Rupununi and the coastal region is cumbersome; this has impeded growth and development. It is against this background that the contribution of the Mother's Union should be assessed. It represents a modest but crucial contribution that facilitates women's movement and activities. It is important to note the Sewing Machine Project in St. John's District of Jawalla in the Mazaruni region.[19] This project enables women to utilize their skills for production of clothes to earn or improve on incomes. Dressmaking has become a viable source of earning income either full time or to supplement incomes. What is important for this study is that the program is providing viable skills and generating income.

Agriculture is the major economic activity of the people of the interior regions. Cooperative ventures were instituted by the union to promote agriculture. Members of the Mother's Union in the District of the Holy Innocents Wowetto have a cooperative farming scheme.[20] Joint ventures provide comradeship and minimize difficulties associated with rural farming in a forest region. Resources are pulled together and moderation enhanced.

Day Care Centers as Supportive Services

Between 1982 and 1989, the Mother's Union established day care centers.[21] Apart from nurturing children in basic Christian ethics and projecting the goals of the Mother's Union, the centers provide support services for working mothers who are compelled by the harsh economic conditions to work outside the home. The responsibility of taking care of children during working hours is allocated for mothers working outside of their home. Women are working either because they are heads of households or, because they are required to supplement incomes. The process of earning incomes and undertaking economic activities either in the formal or informal sector, independently or otherwise, is promoting integration of women in Guyana's development process. In addition and increasingly, women are able to acquire day-care skills through apprenticeship.

Socioeconomic difficulties have been compelling physical emigrations. This is "robbing" Guyana of active population and weakening kinship ties. Kinship ties are crucial and provide support services for people in nonindustrial societies. In industrial societies, technology is sophisticated. Social support services are advanced and automatic and there is less reliance or support of the kin-groups. However, the Mother's Union attempts to fill the gap provided by increasing emigration and declining kinship ties through fostering comradeship and friendship activities among its members. The regular meetings, social functions, mutual aid, and assistance provide emotional, psychological, and material assistance to members. These are considerably supportive especially in times of individual crisis and moments of stress.[22]

The contribution of the Mother's Union is beyond "tokenism". Its scope of activities is broad, affecting women in both rural and urban areas. Exchanges and mutual interdependence are encouraged between rural and urban women. Rural women undertook supplies of food products and crafts to urban women in exchange for such items as clothes and other essential provisions.[23] The impact of the activities of the union is serious. The finances and other resources are considerably limited. Its activities provide necessary stimuli for socio-economic activities which enable women to respond in a positive manner to the pressures of the economic recovery program.

CASWIG (Conference on Affairs and Status of Women in Guyana)

CASWIG is an umbrella organization for nongovernmental voluntary women's associations. It was established in 1976 to coordinate the activities of nongovernmental voluntary associations. Its activities cover 25 voluntary associations. It serves as a resource institution for those associations. The objectives of CASWIG are:

1. To provide communication channels through which women's organizations interact and network

2. Promotion of income generation skills
3. Sensitizing women to their potentials and stimulating their capability to produce and to earn or improve on their incomes
4. To encourage women to be involved in the socioeconomic and political development of Guyana.[24]

The concern of CASWIG is survival of women through diversification of activities of women and accentuating their drive for improved earnings. Like the Mother's Union, it promotes training in traditional skills. But beyond this, it pioneered training of women in nontraditional skills. In general, CASWIG used the same strategies as the Mother's Union — workshops, seminars, and training sessions. In addition, it uses a committee system to carry out its activities.

Training in Nontraditional Female Skills

The objective of this program is to diversify the development and application of the productive energies of women. This broadens the scope of opportunities open to women. For a long time, security services were considered a male preserve. But between 1985 and 1992, CASWIG sponsored the training of 200 women in the Guyana Defense Force (GDF), National Guard, and Police Force as paramilitary personnel.[25] Twenty-five percent of the trainees became self-employed, while 75% are engaged in wage-earning services by security firms. By 1991, 35 women had been trained in the upholstery industry. Eight of this number are self-employed. These activities are radical departures from traditional female engagements. What is important to this work is that security services provide new opportunities for women and enable them to face the effects of the economic recovery pressures positively.

Socioeconomic Service

Staggering inflation has led to a high cost of living. Several mothers are unable to cope with the cost of providing lunch for their children at school. CASWIG attempts to support women and reduce financial strains by undertaking free feeding of school pupils from seriously indigent homes. Proper feeding of school children is considered crucial. Children require certain minimum nutrition to grow mentally and physically and to be able to cope with the demands of school work.

By 1990, the Association was feeding 100 a day and the number rose to 150 by the end of 1991.[26] This number may appear small in relation to the total number of children at school. But the resources of CASWIG are small. The program is functional. It is improving the health and school performance of children.

The Red Thread

This is a voluntary women's association formed in 1986 by a group of women motivated by patriotic zeal of ensuring the survival of women. Its target is rural women. This makes the Red Thread radically different from the two associations already considered. Its emphasis is exploitation and commercialization of existing skills. It strategizes through cooperatives for production. Women with similar skills are formed into cooperatives. One of the important cooperatives is the Embroidery Group.[27] The group produced embroidered items ranging from napkins and decorative pictures to bags and clothes.

The association undertakes marketing and distribution of products. The Guyanese marked is constrained by the low purchasing power of the mass of its people. But there is the prospect for a more active market within the Caribbean region.

Nimbi Project

The economic crisis almost paralyzed the school system. Inflation put the cost of books out of reach for many women.[28] The Nimbi project is concerned with the production of exercise books and other basic textbooks which are distributed to schools for sale to pupils at low cost. Nimbi demonstrates women in action. It is a strategy for dealing with the difficulties and high cost of education in a positive and dynamic manner. The government of Guyana adopted the project because of its viability and attraction. Red Thread is unique in its target and activities. It has undertaken measures that are far from being traditional but which are viable and attractive enough for government adoption. The association symbolizes promise and hope for women and their survival and well-being.

CONCLUSION

This work has demonstrated that since the new economic measures, women's associations have increased in Guyana. All three case studies showed that women have reacted actively to the effects of the Economic Recovery Program. Traditional female pursuits are improved while new ground is broken. The training of women in paramilitary services marks a turning point. The scope of activities for women is expanding.

The provision of general education is a regenerative tool. It eradicates ignorance and created new awareness, consciousness of realities, and potentials hitherto unknown.

Through the associations, women are able to forge relationships that seem to replace declining kinship ties. The demonstration of friendship and fellowship through mutual aid and similar support services provide a "cushion" against stress. By acting in self-interest, Guyanese women are promoting sustenance of families and the welfare of society. The well-being of families is the well-being of society.

In most cases, the associations raise funds independently and internally without reference to government support. They maximize local resources and skills. In some areas they have acted ahead of the government, the latter following the trails blazed by the associations. The Red Thread's Nimbi Project demonstrates this vividly.

Constraints on Women's Activities

Women's activities are constrained by the realities of religion, ethnicity, and tradition. The constraints of tradition are serious in Guyanese society, in particular in the rural area, where women are considered subservient to men. Women who are assertive may be subject to social conflicts in the form of domestic violence and suicide.

Indo-Guyanese women are in most cases non-Christian. They are less likely to become members of organizations that are based on Christian ethics and values. Consequently they may benefit from different kinds of experiences.

Women's actions are also constrained by shortage of funds and other basic resources. Transportation is a major problem. It limits communication and distribution of finished products. The Guyanese women in action provide an attractive example of women's reactions to the pressures of socioeconomic change under economic recovery programs in the Third World. There is a need for international agencies to be more actively involved in the viable projects of women in Guyana.

Women's activities in Guyana are society-oriented. They relate to fundamental issues. Survival is their target. They reach out to the masses of women and the larger population in both rural and urban areas. More women are increasingly engaged in economic pursuits either in the traditional or nontraditional female sectors. New skills are being acquired and women are encroaching on areas formerly dominated by men. In reacting to the harsh effects of the economic recovery measures, women are gradually actualizing themselves.

NOTES

1. C.A. Sunshine, *The Caribbean* (Washington: EPICA, 1988) p. 176.
2. T .J. Spinner Jr., *A Political And Social History of Guyana.* (Boulder: Westview Press, 1984), p. xii.
3. *Ibid.*
4. *Ibid.*
5. T.J. Spinner, *Political and Social History,* p. 206.
6. *Annual Report,* (Georgetown: Bank of Guyana, 1987).
7. *Catholic Standard* 21 Feb 1982.
8. Result of interviews conducted in Guyana, January 1991.
9. *Ibid.*
10. P. Antrobus, "Gender Implications of the Debt Crisis in the Commonwealth Caribbean," Conference of Caribbean Countries, July 1987.
11. See note 8.
12. J. Jackson, *Report on Study of Select Communities in Guyana,* 1990, Women Studies Unit, University of Guyana, 1990.

13. *Ibid.*
14. Jubilee Message, Mother's Union Papers, Georgetown, Guyana 1986.
15. *Annual Reports,* Mother's Union, 1980–1992.
16. *Ibid.*
17. *Ibid.*
18. *Ibid.*
19. Visitations and financial contributions made to individuals in times of crisis.
20. *Ibid.*
21. *Annual Report,* Mother's Union, 1980–1982.
22. *Ibid.*
23. The *UMBRELLA,* August/September 1990, p. 3.
24. The *UMBRELLA,* August 1991, p. 5.
25. *Ibid.*
26. *Ibid.*
27. *Annual Report,* Conference on Affairs and Status of Women in Guyana (CASWIG, 1991).
28. *Reports of Red Thread,* Georgetown, Guyana, 1986–1991.

CHAPTER NINE

POSSIBILITIES FOR CUSHIONING THE ADVERSE EFFECTS OF THE STRUCTURAL ADJUSTMENT PROGRAM ON VULNERABLE WOMEN IN ZAMBIA

MOSEBJANE MALATSI

After a decade of trying without much success to implement structural adjustment programs (SAP) imposed by the World Bank and the International Monetary Fund (IMF), Zambia in May 1987 suspended its relationship with these bodies and introduced, in place of SAP, its own New Economic Recovery Program. However, apparently other multilateral and bilateral donor organizations and development agencies "colluded" with the IMF and World Bank to suspend or reduce their assistance to Zambia and exerted overt pressure on it to resume relations with them.

So Zambia gradually incorporated into its own recovery

program some of the demands of the IMF and World Bank. The Fourth National Development Plan (1989–1993) included some of their measures. The difference was, however, the emphasis on development from Zambia's own resources. The IMF and World Bank began making approving comments on the soundness of the Zambian government's approach, and the gap between them started to narrow.

The second half of 1989 and early 1990 saw various important SAP measures adopted:

- the national currency, the Kwacha, was devalued by more than 100%
- the exchange rate was liberalized and anyone could change hard currency at any bank
- a two-window currency exchange rate was introduced
- prices of all goods and services were decontrolled and subsidies removed, except for maize meal (although its price increased by 60% coupons continued to be issued to people in urban areas as a subsidy)
- fees, though relatively small, were introduced for medical services
- school fees were introduced or increased
- trade barriers were removed

MEASURES TO CUSHION THE EFFECTS OF THE STRUCTURAL ADJUSTMENT PROGRAM ON WOMEN

The above measures were intended to revitalize the economy and reverse the downward trend. In the process, however, prices rocketed, fares increased dramatically, and house rents rose to such a level that many people could not even afford to rent a room. Many poor people could not afford medical and school fees.

Consequently the government decided to lend assistance by cushioning the severe effects of these measures on poor and vulnerable women, including female household heads in the rural areas. Poverty, compounded by the SAP measures aggravated the nutritional state of children from poor households and evidence showed that slightly over 40% of children under five years of age ("under-fives") suffered from malnutrition and related ailments.

The United Nations Development Program (UNDP), Lusaka, responded to the government's appeal and undertook to assess the problem and recommend ways to help affected women meet their food needs and develop income-generating activities. The most severely affected agroecological zones of Zambia were to be identified for such projects.

CRITERIA FOR IDENTIFYING VULNERABLE WOMEN AND THEIR GEOGRAPHIC DISTRIBUTION

The criteria given to the author, in consultation with the UNDP, were as follows:
1. Identify areas of high incidence of malnutrition, ensuring they are representative in terms of rainfall, sociocultural, and cultivation patterns.
2. Review existing projects geared to nutrition in these areas with a view towards identifying nutritional needs not being met, successful projects that could be replicated, and making recommendations for improvement of such projects.
3. Review facilities for improving agricultural production and income-generating activities in terms of their accessibility to women, especially household heads.

Female household heads in rural areas were to be targeted by the study. These women comprised widows, divorced and separated women, single mothers, and women whose husbands were absent for prolonged periods. All were to have children and other dependents to support.

STUDY METHODOLOGY

The study set out to identify rural areas with a high incidence of malnutrition, especially where this affected female-headed households. It was realized that limited resources would necessitate focussing intervention on the most adversely affected areas.

There are three agroecological zones in Zambia, namely:

Zone I: The dry, largely tsetse-infested valleys of the
                 Zambezi and Luangwa Rivers. This zone is
                 found in Eastern, Southern, Lusaka and part of
                 Western Provinces.
Zone IIa/IIb: The moderate rainfall areas of Southern,
                 Lusaka, Central and Eastern Provinces, as well
                 as the Western Provinces.
Zone III: The heavy rainfall area of North Western
                 Province, the Copperbelt, Luapula and Northern
                 Provinces.

COLLECTION AND REVIEW OF REPORTS

Reports and documents on nutrition and maternal health were
collected from the Ministry of Health and on food production
and income-generating activities from the Ministry of
Agriculture.

NUTRITION

Nutritional information was available essentially on children
under five years of age, although there was some on children
between 5 and 14 years. There was next to nothing on adult malnutrition. Maternal health data, though not as comprehensive
as that on children, was the best available indicator on adult
nutrition. It was therefore decided to use information on child
malnutrition to identify the geographic areas most affected.
Although such information was not fully representative of adult
health in the affected areas, it could be inferred that the families of affected children were, *prima facie* at least, not well cared
for nutritionally. While it is possible that food distribution within
households may not be equitable, for Zambia it was thought
unlikely that there would be significant differences between
women and male children.

But, where the food is equitably shared, some household
members, such as children and pregnant or lactating mothers,
require more. Hence, observed malnutrition of up to 40% among
under-fives would show that communities in these areas were
poor, at least in terms of their possession of or ability to buy

nutritious food. Normally, well-off people, in our view, do not suffer from malnutrition. However, in some areas of Zambia it happens that while enough hybrid maize is produced there is malnutrition because it is a cash crop and the money earned from its sale is not used to buy nutritious food for the families of the producer, especially the children.

Table 1.
Nutritionally deficient areas by zone, district, and province

Zone	District	Percentage	Province
I	Gwembe	25-29	Southern
	Mambwe	"	Eastern
IIa	Chama	30-34	Eastern
	Petauke	"	Eastern
	Lundazi	35-39	Eastern
IIb	Senanga	30-34	Western
	Kaoma	"	Western
	Lukulu	35-39	Western
III	Kaputa	35-39	Northern
	Nchelenge	"	Luapula
	Mwense	"	Luapula
	Zambezi	"	N.Western
	Mwinilunga	40 and over	N.Western
	Kasempa	"	N.Western
	Chilubi Island	"	Northern
	Samfya	"	Luapula

Source: National Nutrition Surveillance Program, Ministry of Health, Lusaka, 1987.[1]

The National Nutrition Surveillance Program (NNSP) obtains data from district and provincial hospitals and rural health centers. The general picture of nutrition conveyed was confirmed at meetings with Ministry of Health staff in Lusaka and at the provincial and district levels, although this could not be backed up with statistics.

For instance, except for some areas in the Western Province, there was no data to support the proposition that female household heads cultivated a smaller hectarage and produced less food and cash crops, or that even where they cultivated the same hectarage as men they produced less because they found it harder to procure inputs like fertilizers or hired labor. Nor is there data to support the bias shown by extension staff to male farmers, or to verify that female-headed households are poorer in terms of cash income and material resources.

Yet, from the information provided, it was clear that female household heads had to work harder and longer than their male counterparts and still remained poorer and more vulnerable. They had their household chores, they supervised their children's education and health, collected water and fuel and pounded grain, all in addition to their farming work. They struggled to get land to clear and cultivate, often using only their hand hoes and axes. They had less fertilizer, lower production, and less income to buy additional food to make their meals more nutritious. Hence the increased incidence of malnutrition in their families.

Table 2.
Infant mortality per 1000 live births

Province	Infant Mortality Rate
Luapula	112.12
Eastern	110.08
Western	99.38
Northern	82.87
Southern	76.28
N.Western	71.99
Lusaka	65.22
Central	64.51
Copperbelt	55.66
Total for Zambia	98.67

Source: Zambia Population Census (Lusaka, 1980)[2]

Malnutrition may not be the only cause of these high mortality rates, but malnutrition certainly plays a part in weakening a child and making him or her easy prey to other ailments. Breaking down the data on Luapula Province by sex and residence reveals the following picture:

Table 3.
Infant mortality rates in Luapula Province
by sex and residence

	Rural	Urban	Total
Male	119.3	87.8	113.7
Female	117.4	81.9	110.6

Source: J. Gould, Luapala, Dependence on Development (Zambia: Geographical Association, 1989) p. 30[3]

The National Surveillance Program data for Luapula Province revealed that in the more urban Mansa district, 22% of under-fives were underweight, compared with those in the rural districts of Kawambwa, Mwense, Nchelenge, and Samfya, which registered 32%, 36%, 39%, and 37% of under-fives underweight, respectively.

As Luapula Province "is reported to have the highest natural fertility rate in Zambia,"[4] it is likely that child spacing is not widely practiced, thus leading to early weaning, which in turn contributes to the high infant mortality, as traditional weaning foods are said to be not very nutritious. This situation could be aggravated by the adverse effects of SAP.

FOOD PRODUCTION

Information on food production and income-generating projects was provided by the Ministry of Agriculture in Lusaka and at provincial, districts and subdistrict levels. Unfortunately, little in terms of crops grown, hectarage, or access to extension services was disaggregated by gender. The crop forecasting unit showed the numbers of male and female farmers at district level but not the hectarage cultivated or the types of crops and the yield. In the absence of such differentiated data, one could not conclusively say that female farmers were worse off. However, our informants emphasized that female farmers were cultivating a smaller hectarage and producing less crops than male farmers. The data provided by K.C. Chileya and G.A. Vierstra confirmed this.[5]

In both patrilineal and matrilineal societies, property used by an individual is taken over at his or her death by the kin group because, in the final analysis it is the kin group that is the absolute owners of property. This explains the low percentage of plots given out by husbands to their wives, for they belong to different kin groups. According to the 1980 Census of Population and Housing, the average household size was five people. Female-headed households had an average size of 4.1 individuals as compared with 5.3 for male-headed households. They thus had fewer male adults and lack of labor power was a severe constraint.[6]

Table 4.

Percentage distribution of households by sex of head, province and residence, 1969–1980

	TOTAL		RURAL	URBAN
	1969	1980	1980	1980
	Male/Female	Male/Female	Male/Female	Male/Female
All Provinces	76.2/23.8	72.3/27.7	67.3/32.7	82.1/17.9
Central	80.2/19.8	78.4/21.6	76.7/23.3	82.4/17.6
Copperblt	90.4/ 9.6	85.8/14.2	78.2/21.8	88.0/12.0
Eastern	64.0/36.0	62.4/37.6	61.1/38.9	78.2/21.8
Luapula	66.0/34.0	64.0/35.8	63.3/36.7	72.0/28.0
Lusaka	88.2/11.8	79.2/20.8	71.8/28.2	81.2/18.8
Northern	61.4/38.6	63.1/36.9	62.8/37.2	64.3/35.7
N.Western	75.7/24.3	69.0/31.0	68.5/31.5	72.5/27.5
Southern	82.9/17.1	74.9/25.1	73.2/26.8	80.0/20.0
Western	72.9/26.1	64.0/36.0	63.1/36.9	69.4/30.6

Source: Zambian Popluation Census (Lusaka, 1980). 1969 data not classified by residence.[7]

The percentage and distribution of female-headed households has probably not changed seriously since 1980, though it may have increased in rural areas, as more males than females have been migrating to the urban areas. But, although more than one in every three households in the rural areas is headed by a woman, they are not concentrated in one spot so it would not be feasible to target projects at them specifically. Our proposal was to ensure that projects included all the female-headed households in the project area.

Some provinces are self-sufficient in food and others have to import food. Female-headed households in the latter are likely to be hardest hit by the structural adjustment programs. Luapula and Western Province are food deficient, and female-headed households in these provinces are likely to be harder hit than their counterparts in Eastern and Northern Provinces, where food surpluses are produced.

Social, cultural, and traditional cultivation patterns are strongly influenced by agroecology and the environment. For instance, in Zone I, the cultivation of crops was almost exclusively by traditional tools such as handhoes, axes, cutlasses, etc., since most of the area was infested by tsetse fly, and cattle could not be kept. Few people could afford tractors for ploughing. The majority of people in Zone I, especially female household heads, could only cultivate a small hectarage and thus realized low levels of food production and cash crops.

Women in general, and women household heads in particular, had difficulty obtaining credit, which meant they used inadequate fertilizer. Most women in Zone I cultivated maize, sorghum, and, in a few places, cassava and millet. They also grew groundnuts, sunflowers, and sweet potatoes for their families' own use and occasionally engaged in selling to generate income. Cotton was also grown in Zone I, but very little of it was grown by female household heads because of credit problems and their neglect by extension services.

In most of Zone IIb, cattle were kept for draught power and other purposes. However, traditionally in Lozi culture women are not allowed to handle cattle and they were obliged to hire male labor to use the animals and manure their fields. This hindered female household heads as they could not afford hired help.

Traditional cultivation practices in Zone II were until recently characterized by slash-and-burn methods using an axe and hand hoe. This is still used to a limited extent. Animal power is a recent introduction, and those who can *hire* tractors for ploughing do so. There are training programs on the use of oxen for drought power, but few women participate in them as yet. Since cattle culture is not yet deeply ingrained in Luaula's tradition, it would be advisable to involve women at this stage — so they are not relegated to the background as they are in other parts of Zambia — so the use of animal power does not become a male domain only.

AGROECOLOGICAL ZONES THAT SHOULD BE TARGETED

The areas with more than 40% of under-fives affected by malnutrition were in Luapula and North Western Provinces. Luapula and Western Province were areas of serious food (maize) deficiency. At the top of the list of provinces with high percentages of female-headed households was the Eastern Province, followed by Western, Northern, and Luapula Provinces. The areas covered by rail lines, so that Southern, Lusaka, Central and Copperbelt Provinces are comparatively well developed, less adversely affected by malnutrition, and have a lower level of female headed households. There is sufficient food, so intervention was less urgently needed.

It was decided that priority should be given to Luapula and North Western Provinces, in agroecological Zone III.

The central focus of intervention should be nutrition, linked to food availability, accessibility, and affordability.

In advocating gender-sensitive handling of issues arising from SAP, Collier observes that, in earning income, women face different constraints.[8] Since structural adjustment is about changing constraints, men and women should be treated as distinct groups. Further, men and women consume public services differently and, hence, budgetary changes have gender-differentiated effects. Women household heads experience additional problems because of the limitations imposed on them by society in terms of obtaining land, credit, employment, and extension services, and they are overburdened by household chores and responsibilities.

Because no government or other agency is addressing all these areas as they affect vulnerable groups of women, the proposed projects would need to have an interagency, integrated, multisectoral approach in addressing the following issues:

- food production, processing and storage
- nutrition, health education, and child and maternal health
- income generation, credit provision, marketing, and cooperatives
- organizational and technical skills training
- institution building to facilitate popular participation
- short-term intervention measures to cushion the adverse effects of structural adjustment
- long-term sustainability and the continuous improvement of the quality of life of affected women

CONCLUSION

Structural Adjustment Programs have adverse effects. The hardest hit are the poor and vulnerable, of which households headed by women form a substantial part.

To cushion the negative effects of structural adjustment on this group, the government of Zambia appealed to the UNDP to develop appropriate productive and processing projects.

The UNDP assessed the situation of this group in all provinces and selected those districts most severely affected by child malnutrition for project implementation.

NOTES

1. M. Chirwa, *National Nutrition Surveillance Program (NNSP)*, (Lusaka: Ministry of Health, 1989).
2. Zambian Population Census (Lusaka, 1980).
3. J. Gould, *Luapula, Dependence or Development*, (Zambia: Geographical Association, 1989).
4. *Ibid.* p. 28.
5. K. Chileya and G. Vierstra, *Information about Female Headed Household*, (Mongu: Adaptive Research Planning Team (ARPT), 1990).
6. *Ibid.*
7. Zambian Population Census (Lusaka, 1980).

8. P. Collier, "SDA Analysis Plan, Gender-specific Issues in the Analysis of Survey Data," (Oxford: Institute of Economics and Statistics, 1990).

CHAPTER 10

ECONOMIC CRISIS, STRUCTURAL ADJUSTMENT AND AFRICA'S FUTURE

Julius O. Ihonvbere

The current African crisis is not just a narrow economic crisis but also fundamentally a political crisis. Besides the usual political instability or crisis of legitimacy, this political crisis is reflected in the pervasive lack of democracy, which some perceive as a conflict between state and people's power — a crisis arising from lack of popular participation in the development process.[1]

In the decades to come Africa is likely to witness frequent and devastating drought and famine, increasingly rapid rates of desertification, epidemics, plagues of locusts and other such calamities. As a result the political climate is likely to become hotter and more difficult for those in power.[2]

The vast majority of nations in Sub-Saharan Africa are currently implementing structural adjustment programs (SAPs). The achievements have been very modest and in most cases tenuous.[3] There is agreement, however, on the social, political, and economic tensions, coalitions, and conflicts which SAPs have generated. In Zaire, Zambia, and Nigeria, to name a few, adjustment programs have accentuated the delegitimization of the state, led to political violence, riots, and regime turnover and culminated in severe economic dislocation and deterioration. It is the position of the Organization of African Unity (OAU) that even the efforts of the United Nations to support the restructuring process through the United Nations Programme of Action for African Economic Recovery and Development(UNPAAERD) "did not witness any significant change for the better in Africa....from all economic indicators, the continent of Africa appeared to have been by-passed by [the] positive developments in the world system."[4] The harsh monetarist prescriptions of the International Monetary Fund (IMF) and the World Bank have not restored investor confidence in African economies and they have not reduced the foreign debt profiles or promoted foreign exchange earnings. On the contrary, African states have dismantled all the political, economic, and social gains of the past three decades, accumulated more foreign debts, and exposed their respective economies to foreign penetration, domination, and exploitation.

There are some very visible impacts and implications of structural adjustment which would no doubt affect the location and role of Africa in the global division of labor and determine the context of class contradictions and struggles in the 1990s:

1. Adjustment has delegitimized the state, thus eroding its tenuous hegemony.
2. It has increased the alienation of the people from the agents and agencies of the state.
3. It has intensified class contradictions and struggles, proletarianized the middle classes, and further impoverished the lower classes.
4. It has increased the social and eonomic burdens of vulnerable groups — women, youths, children, and the unem-

ployed, and simply made life difficult for these groups.

5. It has created severe economic dislocations — i.e. higher debts, rising debt-servicing ratios, inflation, scarcity of essential goods, unemployment, devalued currencies, and agricultrural stagnation.

6. It has increased the degradation of the environment by forcing the elites into all sorts of extralegal ways of making money, including the importation of toxic wastes, and by compelling the poor to abuse their environment in the struggle to make a living by exploiting natural resources without regard for conservation.

7. It has promoted social decay, violence, cynicism and uncertainty, petty-crime, prostitution, armed robbery, drug-use and drug-trafficking, corruption, currency laundering, and the like.

8. It has made African economies more vulnerable to foreign penetration, manipulation, exploitation and domination, as international finance institutions, donors, and Western governments have now taken on the direct and/or indirect responsibility for dictating political and economic policies and models for African states.

9. It has fostered the intensification of repression, political intolerance, and human rights abuses in the effort to convince investors that the state was "really in charge" and had popular forces under control and in the effort to force orthodox adjustment policies on the people, their organizations, and society without mechanisms for equitably redistributing power, resuorces, or the pains and gains of restructuring.

10. It has precipitated a massive and unprecedented "brain-drain" to Europe, North America, and the Middle East, due to unemployment, repression, and the need to escape the pains of adjustment. In this regard "Africa has lost a third of its skilled people to Europe" alone, according to the United Nations Development Programme (UNDP's) *Human Development Index* for 1992.[5]

It is only in the context of these and other consequences of structural adjustment in Africa that we can effectively make projections as to the future of Africa and the future of adjustment

in Africa. In the rest of this chapter, we look first at the implications of orthodox structural adjustment for state and society
in Africa; second, at why adjustment has failed in Africa; and,
thirdly, at the new global order, adjustment, and the future of
Africa.

IMPLICATIONS OF ADJUSTMENT
FOR STATE AND SOCIETY

There is now almost unanimous agreement among intellectuals
and policy-makers in and outside the African continent that
orthodox adjustment programs as devised and supervised by
the IMF and the World Bank are not working.[6] At a more general level, attention has recently become focused on the negative consequences of adjustment programs which do not pay
particular attention to existing socioeconomic and political
inequalities in underdeveloped social formations. M. de
Larosiere, managing director of the IMF, has equally argued that
public support is essential for the success of adjustment programs and that if there are "no pay-offs in terms of growth...while
human conditions are deteriorating," it would be impossible to
continue the adjustment program. He concluded that "human
capital is after all the most important factor of production."[7] This
realization did not in any way encourage a fundamental change
in the prescriptions of the IMF restructuring processes in underdeveloped countries. The UNDP's *Human Development Report
1990* is clear on the fact that "structural adjustment programmes...have increased the burden of poverty of recipient
nations and their people."[8] In its two-volume study of the
impacts of structural adjustment programs in the Third World,
Adjustment with a Human Face, the UNICEF drew attention to
the need to include "poverty alleviation" programs in adjustment packages if they are not to cause more problems than
envisaged by policy makers.[9]

Specifically in the case of Africa, attacks against structural
adjustment have arisen not from opposition to the need for
change, but from a recognition of the negative political, economic, and social contradictions and conflicts which the program has tended to accentuate or generate. Carol Lancaster

argued in a recent study of adjustment in Sub-Saharan Africa that by 1983 "it had become clear that few of the nearly 20 agreements between the IMF and the African governments had been successful."[10] She also took the position that the IMF adjustment model "has almost never worked in Sub-Saharan Africa."[11] In 1988, the United Nations Programme of Action for African Economic Recovery and Development (UNPAAERD), in its continent-wide review of adjustment programs, conceded that there were a few gains in "a handful of countries...in certain macroeconomic indicators" such as reduced inflation rates and higher export volumes. It concluded, however, that "for the majority of African states, there has not been even a hint of recovery."[12] Claude Ake has noted that adjustment programs are being pursued by African states in a "desperate attempt to contain the crisis (of the continent) and save the state." However, he argues that policies of "massive retrenchment of public employees, the withdrawal of government subsidies, and the dismantling of welfare schemes, the privatization of public corporations, the deindigenization of the economy...are replete with contradictions and address the symptoms and not the causes of the problems." It is Ake's contention that adjustment programs will inevitably deepen the crisis of the continent, because they address neither the specificities and implications of the historical experiences of African countries nor the content and character of contemporary politics, political balances, and struggles:

> [The] withdrawal of welfare measures, minimal in the first place, in a context where the most elementary needs are lacking only intensifies the contradictions between the rulers and the subordinate classes. And so does the mass retrenchment of workers. Privatization can only deepen the class contradictions for it is bound to mean the cheap sale of public stock to the few who are already well-off; the attempt to make public corporations efficient and profitable cannot work because the political class must continue to use them as a means of accumulation; deindigenization of the economy entails the strengthening of those exploitative ties and the dependence which under-

lies underdevelopment. In any case, destatization can only go so far because the objective conditions which produce statism remain as strong as they have always been.[13]

Ake's position was supported by the United Nations Economic Commission for Africa (ECA) when it argued in its *Economic Report on Africa 1990* that "policy prescriptions widely adopted during the decade (1980-1990), based on conventional adjustment programmes, have failed to address the fundamental structural issues in Africa's development; hence their failure to arrest the downward trend, less reverse it and bring about a sustainable process of development and transformation."[14] Adebayo Adedeji, as executive secretary of the ECA, was quite direct in his opposition to the adjustment program when he noted that "on-going SAPs" have led to a situation in which "enormous social costs have been imposed on the vulnerable segments of the population; the human resources for transformation are crippled; domestic structural inequalities increase and the marginalization of Africa proceeds apace."[15] Finally, in a surprising though not unexpected move, the World Bank shifted some distance away from the IMF when in its 1989 report on Africa it admitted its own past failures in Africa and embraced the call for protecting vulnerable groups, empowerment of the people, democratization, and adjustment with a human face:

> It is not sufficient for African governments merely to consolidate the progress made in their adjustment programs. They need to go beyond the issues of public finance, monetary policy, prices, and markets to address fundamental questions relating to human capacities, institutions, governance, the environment, population growth and distribution, and technology. Changes in perceptions and priorities, as well as in incentives, will be required to bring about improvements. Above all, to channel the energies of the population at large, ordinary people should participate more in designing and implementing development programs.[16]

It is obvious therefore that structural adjustment programs

forced on African states by mounting problems and deepening socioeconomic and political contradictions have not achieved the goals set by the IMF and the World Bank, i.e., increased production, investment, and growth, achieved through the efficient use of resources. More importantly, orthodox adjustment programs have destroyed the social fabric of African societies, promoted a culture of corruption, cynicism, and crass individualism; taken corruption and violence to unprecedented levels; and delegitimized the state in a devastating manner.

Why have these adjustment programs, in spite of vitriolic propaganda,[17] failed generally in Africa? In the next section we argue that adjustment programs have failed for several reasons: the way in which the African crisis was defined; the central concerns of the adjustment package; and the character of politics and political power in the continent.

WHY STRUCTURAL ADJUSTMENT FAILED IN AFRICA

We noted above that adjustment programs have a limited chance of success if they fail to take proper cognizance of existing socioeconomic and political power balances and contradictions. The fact remains that ultimately, it is the internal character of power, politics, and social relations that determine and influence the ability of the government to implement the often harsh prescriptions of the IMF and the World Bank. African governments and the ECA are agreed that some adjustment is inevitable in the face of the current crisis and further marginalization in the global system. The disagreement is on the content, context, relevance, and manageability of the adjustment program.

Eboe Hutchful has provided an outline of issue areas to be considered in the implementation of adjustment programs in view of the "significant implications for the reproductive space and dynamics of political regimes."[18] Though Hutchful concentrates on Ghana, in this section, we shall draw examples from the Nigerian experience with structural adjustment. The first issue area is the depth of the preadjustment crisis as well as the "rate and severity of the decline" before adjustment. In the case of Ghana the economy was already in ruins, and hardship had become part of the people's reality. The harshness of the IMF and World Bank prescriptions, therefore, made very little difference to the people. In Nigeria, the reverse was the case. The oil boom had given the impression that the problem was with how to spend the money, not with how to generate it. By 1986, when the adjustment package was introduced, most Nigerians were of the view that the setbacks were going to be temporary; after all, the country was still in the oil-producing business. What this means is that the point at which adjustment is introduced and the severity of the policies must pay due cognizance to the existing preparedness of the people to withstand the pains of restructuring. Hence, in Ghana, opposition was not as violent and persistent as it has been in Zambia and Nigeria.

A second critical issue area is the degree of adjustment required for recovery. The lending institutions have tended to impose very harsh conditionalities on African countries — conditionalities which pay very little regard to the structural differences, regime types, and opportunities for manoeuvre internally and externally. As Hutchful has rightly noted, "almost all African programs belong in the high conditionality end of the scale," and this situation implies that regimes have less room to set their "own reform agenda and construct the appropriate coalitions."[19] This has been another major source of opposition to structural adjustment in Africa. The package is seen as foreign-formulated, foreign-inspired, and foreign-imposed in a grand strategy to recolonize the continent under the supervision of the IMF and the World Bank. Because of the stringency of the conditionalities, African regimes have had very limited room for "domesticating" their packages, and local innovations easily become incorporated into set patterns handed down by the lending bodies. Though the Nigerian military junta started off pretending to incorporate public interests in the process of adjustment, it ended up in succumbing to all the dictates of the Fund and the Bank.

Third, is the external environment which affects the ability to draw international support, resources, and technical assistance to mediate the harshness of adjustment in conditions of poverty and underdevelopment? With the changes in Eastern Europe and the apparent redirection of international interest and support away from Africa, this becomes an even more pressing issue. The record of waste, mismanagement, and widespread corruption in African states have contributed immensely to eroding possible support from the international environment.[20] Thus, we now begin to hear of "aid fatigue" and "compassion fatigue" in the international community. In reality, these are mere excuses to justify declining assistance, investments, and the redirection of political and economic aid to Eastern Europe and parts of the Middle East.

The fourth issue area is the "nature of national constituencies and sociopolitical actors, their composition, interests, tolerance thresholds, their 'discourse of resistance', and ability to resist adjustment,"[21] which are of utmost importance to the success of adjustment. Unfortunately, the lending agencies have over the years tended to treat these matters, critical as they are, rather lightly. Specifically, this point is about the track record of the dominant elites, the character of their politics, their ability to reproduce themselves through the careful manipulation of power and ideological discourses, the dominant world-view, their relations to nonbourgeois forces, the character of their relation to foreign interests, the use to which they put the state, and their pattern of production and accumulation. In Africa, the dominant elites are mostly responsible for the deepening crisis today through their records of waste, corruption, nepotism, and commitment to the reproduction of unequal exchange relations with foreign capital. As well, their tenuous relation to production has contributed significantly to the expansion of the bureaucracy, parastatals, and commerce, and the stagnation of productive activities. The Nigerian example is of particular relevance. The bourgeoisie has never been known, until relatively recently, to be interested in production; even so, this is hardly a major preoccupation of the burgeois class. The state has always been a means to capital accumulation. The hegemony of the dominant classes has always been tenuous and it has, since political independence, relied on the manipulation of religion, ethnicity, and region to retain political dominance and win access to the state.

The bourgeoisie has always been concentrated in the real estate, service, and import-export sectors of the economy as against involvement in agriculture and other productive activities. Finally, its factionalization and fractionalization, inability to build hegemony, its corruption, and incapacity to effectively manage society and improve on the living conditions of the majority has alienated the people from the state and its agents and agencies. When such a dominant elite comes up with harsh monetarist policies, it cannot mobilize support for it. Rather, it will ignite opposition, and even riots against its programs. Hence, in Nigeria, Zambia, and Cote d'Ivoire, adjustment programs have been met with strong opposition from the people, who see them as another attempt by the dominant elites to make life difficult for the poor.

Hutchful introduces another very critical issue area for consideration when he talks of "regime dynamics": the composition and character of ruling coalitions; mechanisms for securing "vertical and horizontal solidarities;" nature of political discourses and the "relationship between technocrats and politicians, and between political and technocratic rationality and decision-making centers in individual regimes, and in particular the autonomy and insulation from political pressures enjoyed by the technocratic staff."[22] Again, lending agencies hardly go beyond the surface in their negotiations with African power elites for adjustment support. Where the bourgeoisie has historically depended on the state for largesse or accumulation, adjustment is unlikely to be palatable to it. Policies which emphasize financial rationality, accountability, and discipline are usually resisted by elites who are used to accumulation through inflated contracts, stealing from public coffers, using public positions for accumulation, and relying on connections with public officers to get rich. This has been the case in Nigeria. If stabilization makes it more difficult for the elites to accumulate through access to the state, the whole process of corruption can become more desperate and brazen. This only erodes the effectiveness of the adjustment package and reduces the credibility of the political elites, who impose harsh policies on the people and turn around to loot public resources without restraint in order to maintain their preadjustment life styles. While adjustment packages usually demand devaluation, desubsidization, deregulation, privatization, and the general withdrawal of the state from economic activities, such recommendations not only run contrary to the expectations of African peoples but often address the wrong issues. The focus is often on state intervention, not on the character and nature of the intervention. Even in the advanced capitalist societies, the state is still very prominent in promoting private accumulation and in protecting the poor and disadvantaged through health subsidies, unemployment insurance, cheap housing, subsidized public transportation, and even free primary education, with hundreds of thousands of fellowships and scholarships for higher education. This is precisely what African peoples expect of their governments. However, adjustment has meant higher food prices, stagnating incomes, devalued wages and salaries, scarcity of essential goods, inflation, retrenchment of workers, imposition of user-fees on social services, higher cost of education, and higher house rents for workers. These policies have tended to generate opposition to the state and adjustment while leading to riots by the populace and repression by the state in the effort by its custodians to hold on to state power. Without doubt, the "neoclassical basis of structural adjustment" as outlined above, "contradicts...the tenets of nationalism, statism, and welfarism and their embedded notions of entitlements which are central to many African regimes".[23] National development programs and public statements by African leaders since political independence in the 1960s have focused on the need for mobilization and the responsibility of the state to cater for the needs of the majority in society. This was also one of the cardinal points raised by the nationalists in the struggle for political independence. Under adjustment, African regimes are now compelled to go against all the promises they had made to the people over the years. It becomes very difficult to push through a completely different set of prescriptions which go directly against the tenets of nationalism and welfarism which are still strongly enshrined in African culture and value systems. As well, internal factionalization and fractionalization pose major challenges to the success of adjustment. Bureaucrats tend to support adjustment; they have to implement them any way. Not all factions of the officer corps in the armed forces support adjustment, hence it has become one major excuse for coups and counter-coups. In Nigeria, both the Vatsa coup of 1986 and the Orka coup of 1990 were opposed to structural adjustment. While a fraction of the bourgeoisie in league with foreign capital might support adjustment, local investors are often in opposition because floating interest rates and devaluation make it difficult to borrow, lower wages depress the buying power of workers, and trade liberalization removes all the protection they previously enjoyed against imports. Politicians are often divided into three groups — those who support adjustment wholeheartedly; those who oppose adjustment from a populist angle so as to win the support of nonbourgeois forces in their political objectives; and third, those who oppose adjustment purely from a nationalistic position. Such divisions make it difficult for the government to effectively mediate or contain popular pressures and maintain a steady course on the implementation of adjustment programs. Of course, the fluidities of national solidarities which accompany intensifying intra- and inter-class divisions equally impede the ability of the regime to confront societal crisis in a holistic fashion while responding to the urgent demands of social interests within the limits of available resources.

The "moral and political credibility of the leadership (the perception that the leadership is not personally corrupt and can be relied upon to decide wisely in the national interest)" as well as its ability to play constituency against constituency, juggle accountability to international interests and national constituencies, "create a 'discourse of reform' and effectively exploit political symbolism"[24] and its skill in sharing the costs of adjustment between interest groups can make a major difference to the implementation of adjustment. Lending institutions waste their time when they expect leaders who are generally perceived by their people to be untrustworthy, corrupt, inept, and unjust to implement even harsher policies than those which already alienate the people from them. In the case of Ghana, Jerry Rawlings had a good rapport with the left, students, and academics (at least initially), he had the legacy of Kwame Nkrumah

and the socialist rhetoric of the early days of political independence to rely on, and given the very vibrant intellectual culture
of the country, it was easy to get the people to debate and experiment, even at the grassroots level, with ideological positions
previously debated in the university campuses. The reverse was
the case in Nigeria. Ibrahim Babangida declared a "war" against
trade unions, students, and the left. He declared them extrem-
ists and barred them from the political process. He proscribed
trade unions, rehabilitated disgraced and discredited politicians
and military men, and had no patience with ideological dis-
cussions. Babangida also lacked any national symbols, he
accentuated the retreat into ethnic, regional, and religious bases
of acquiring and using political power, shielded corrupt public
officials from punishment, and has himself been accused of corrupt practices. The point therefore was that he was not trusted.
The numerous debates he sponsored on housing, foreign policy,
political restructuring, and so on, were perceived as diversions
and his tendency to accumulate excessive powers to himself and
his office convinced many Nigerians that he could not be trusted
or relied upon to lead the country out of its economic predica-
ment.[25] More importantly, the Babangida regime has been
unable to share the costs of adjustment equally; a few rich have
become super-rich as contractors, military officers, and top
bureaucrats, and their friends collaborate to enrich themselves
while the majority are subjected to retrenchment and other harsh
consequences of the adjustment program. He has therefore
found it very difficult to mobilize and retain the support of critical social actors. Under such conditions adjustment can make
little progress and often remains bogged down to financial
manipulations with the *structures* not experiencing any adjustment.[26]

The point remains that the more repressive and undemocratic
a regime is, the less its chances of effectively implementing
adjustment programs. Repression and human rights violation
encourage opposition elements to develop concrete political programs to oppose the regime. One way of advancing the interest
of the opposition is to discredit and where possible sabotage the
policies of the government, and adjustment programs are easy

targets in this area. A more open and democratic regime — compare Rawlings in Ghana, even now, to Babangida in Nigeria — can convince the people to make sacrifices; convince the people that there is hope in the future, and convince external supporters that it is not only in command but has the support of the people in the process of change, no matter how painful. Coalitions, conflicts, and contradictions are easily managed or mediated, and organized interest groups — in particular, the labor unions and students as well as peasants and local investors — give support and openly defend adjustment policies in the collective effort to find solutions to the deepening crisis. This is possible only where the regime is fairly institutionalized, enjoys some credibility, is not steeped in corruption, and is capable of accommodating alternative positions and interpretations of the path to progress and reform.

THE NEW GLOBAL ORDER, ADJUSTMENT, AND THE FUTURE

Monumental changes have taken place in the global system in the last decade or so. From the crumbling of the Berlin Wall and the reunification of Germany, through the disintegration of the Soviet Union as a nation and superpower, to the emergence of the United States as the sole superpower and the release of Nelson Mandela in South Africa, the world is experiencing a restructuring of global political and economic relations. The net implication of these changes for Africa is that it is going to be increasingly pressured to adopt market reforms in the context of the triumph of the market all over the world, even in communist China. As well, Africa is being marginalized, investors are divesting from Africa and reinvesting in Eastern Europe, donors are complaining of aid-and-compassion fatigue; and responses to political conflicts, famine, and natural disasters have been left largely to voluntary humanitarian bodies. While these conditions of neglect, disinterest, and marginalization may appear rather unfavorable to Africa, they do contain possibilities for mapping out an alternative path to growth, development, and democracy. This is the opportune moment for Africa to face up to the challenges of the present and plan for the future. The so-called new world order makes little or no room for Africa, except those nations that are of some importance to centers of imperialism. How has Africa responded to these developments?

In February 1990 the ECA, with the support of African governments and UN agencies, produced the *African Charter for Popular Participation in Development* as a document to promote the operationalization of the *African Alternative Framework to Structural Adjustment Programme* and the World Bank's recent publication, *Sub-Saharan Africa — From Crisis to Sustainable Growth.*[27] The ECA's alternative framework agreed on the need for adjustment but disagreed on the undue emphasis on financial matters, unrestricted rolling back of the state, blanket privatization, devaluation, and liberalization. More importantly, it argued that adjustment programs stood little chances of success with the impoverishment of the people, their marginalization and repression. The World Bank's report moved from its traditional position of focusing purely on economic matters to admitting its own shortcomings as an organization, emphasizing the need for popular participation in decision-making, decentralization of power structures, accountability, some role for the state in the economy, empowerment of popular organizations, the need for "special measures...to alleviate poverty and protect the vulnerable,"[28] and the need for structures to enable "ordinary people" to "participate more in designing and implementing development programs."[29] With these new positions, even if superficial, the ECA came up with a charter to operationalize the new emphasis on empowerment and democratization. Though the document is still far from perfect and contains some of the usual apologetic and overtly optimistic expectations which fail to take cognizance of entrenched class interests in African states, it represents a new reality in articulating options to the crisis.

The *African Charter*, in asserting the role of popular participation in the economic recovery process, stated clearly that the present crisis "is not only an economic crisis but also a human, legal, political and social crisis" which is "unprecedented and unacceptable" because it is manifested "tragically and glaringly in the suffering, hardship and impoverishment of the vast majority of African people." Perhaps this definition of the character of the crisis is the most important contribution of the document. What it does is to call on policy makers in and outside Africa to look at the crisis from a holistic, but especially political dimension rather than just as a balance-of-payments crisis and so on. It is in line with this perspective that the Charter insists that "there must be an opening up of political process to accommodate freedom of opinions, tolerate differences, accept consensus on issues as well as ensure the effective participation of the people and their organizations and associations." It therefore makes specific prescriptions at the levels of the people; students; youths; non-governmental organizations (NGOs), and voluntary development organizations (VDOs); the media; the government; and the international community to ensure the attainment of the goals of empowerment and democratization.

At the level of government, for instance, the document insists that, as a starting point, African governments must begin to "adopt development strategies, approaches and programmes, the content and parameters of which are in line with the interest and aspirations of the people and which incorporate, rather than alienate, African values and economic, social, cultural, political and environmental realities." In addition, it calls on governments to pursue development objectives with the interests of the people in mind, with emphasis on "popular participatory process... which aim at transformation of the African economies to achieve self-reliant and self-sustaining people-centred development based on popular participation and democratic consensus." To achieve these goals, more economic power must be extended to the people through equitable income distribution, support for their productive capacity, enhanced access to land, credit, technology and information; the protection of children; promotion of the role of women; promotion of literacy and skills training; greater participation and consensus building; elimination of laws and bureaucratic obstacles which militate against development and people's participation; increased employment opportunities for the rural and urban poor; strengthening small scale indigenous entrepreneurship and intensifying efforts at promoting effective subregional and regional economic cooperation. Of course, nothing like these exist presently in any African country, perhaps on paper in the former socialist-inclined countries. If such policies were in place and were pursued with some degree of seriousness, the current crisis would not have come about in the first place. With entrenched social divisions and interests, there are certainly fundamental obstacles to getting African leaders and decision-makers who have over the decades monopolized decision-making and the singular rights, along with politicians, to allocate resources and determine the direction of growth and development.

At the international level, the *Charter* calls for support in Africa's "drive to internalize the development and transformation process." In particular, the IMF, World Bank, and other bilateral and multilateral donors are called upon to "accept and support African initiatives to conceptualize, formulate and implement endogenously designed development and transformation programmes." To achieve these goals, technical assistance should be directed at strengthening national capabilities for policy analysis and the design and implementation of economic reform and development programs. The decentralization of the development process must be supported in order to foster the democratization of development; the new emphasis on popular empowerment, "active participation of the people and their organizations in the formulation of development strategies and economic reform programmes and open debate and consensus-building process" need to be given full support and the reduction of the stock of Africa's debt and debt-servicing obligations should be given urgent attention.

Addressing the place of women in the unfolding political struggles in Africa, the *Charter* comes out clearly to reinforce the provisions of the 1989 Abuja Declaration on Women and notes that the new partnership required to transform the region "must not only recognize the importance of gender issues but must take action to ensure women's involvement at all levels of decision-making." It specifically calls on all African governments to "set ... specific targets for the appointment of women in senior policy and management posts in all sectors of government."[30] The document calls on women and their organizations to continue to "strive for the attainment of policies and programmes that reflect and recognize women's roles as producers, mothers, active community mobilizers and custodians of culture" and advocates gender equality at home, at the work place, and in society in general.

Specifically on adjustment programs, the *Charter* is emphatic on the point that:

> ...the human dimension is central to adjustment programmes which must be compatible with the objectives and aspirations of the African people and with African realities and must be conceived and designed internally by African countries as part and parcel of the long term objectives and framework of development and *transformation*.[31]

Finally, the international community is called upon to give direct support to grassroots organization, trade unions, women's and youth's organizations, and NGOs in their training, networking, and other activities.

In spite of these seemingly attractive pleas and declarations, it would be inappropriate not to highlight the obstacles to Africa's recovery. As it stands, the IMF has shifted no ground in its conceptualization and interpretation of the African crisis. Its prescriptions are still the same and it has little room for concern about the human cost of structural adjustment. Its commitment to monetarism remains unshaken. Though the World Bank made significant concessions in 1989 by emphasising political conditionality, empowerment, democratization, and accountability, it has yet to demonstrate this new shift in practice. As Robert Browne has noted, "merely because the forces of enlightenment succeeded in obtaining publication of the document does not guarantee that the bureaucracy will be mobilized to implement it — a task which would be Herculean even with the best of intentions."[32] As well, international banking institutions have yet to demonstrate their recognition of Africa's specificities and peculiarities within the underdeveloped world. It cannot be expected, therefore, that the *Charter's* call on the international community and on African governments will be heeded in the very near future — not at least, until serious internal restructuring takes place within the continent to encourage donors, lenders, and the international community to take a second look at Africa. Yet, we can conclude that the negative consequences of structural adjustment policies in Africa have helped to significantly encourage challenges to the state and its custodians; and has promoted an unprecedented alliance between popular groups. The new struggles for empowerment, social justice, human rights, political participation, the decentralization of decision-making, and multi-party politics cannot be stopped. The ongoing changes, even in the most hardcore repressive nations like Kenya and Zaire, cannot be stopped. Whatever the gains of the ongoing struggles, the fact remains that:

> The new democratic governments, or those retained after honest elections, will be confronted with the difficult challenge of reviving stagnant economies. In most cases, they will inherit depleted treasuries, high debt repayments, declining earnings from commodity exports, low levels of private investments and increased dependence on international aid and loans....[33]

Beyond structural adjustment, beyond the positions of the IMF and the World Bank, and beyond the changes in the global system, the challenge for popular forces and their organizations in the 1990s will be to survive the pressures in the emerging global system, and to sustain the drive for a stronger civil society and democracy in the context of deepening systemic crisis.

NOTES

1. Adebayo Adedeji, "Development and Ethics: Putting Africa on the Road to Self-Reliant and Self-Sustaining Process of Development," Keynote address delivered at the first plenary session of the Thirty-third Annual Meeting of the African Studies Association, Baltimore, Maryland, November 1–4, 1990.
2. Adotey Bing, "Salim A. Salim on the OAU and the African Agenda," *Review of African Political Economy* 50 (March 1991):63.

3. See Adebayo Adedeji,"Economic Progress: What Africa Needs," *Transafrica Forum* 7, 2 (Summer 1990): 11–26.
4. Chu Okongwu, Nigeria's Minster for Budget and Planning, speaking on behalf of the OAU at the Review of UNPAAERED, New York, September 3-13, 1992. Reproduced in *Africa Recovery* 5, 4 (December 1991).
5. Quoted from "Improved 'Global Governance' Demanded," *Africa Recovery* (August 1992):13.
6. See: World Bank, *Sub-Saharan Africa: From Crisis to Sustainable Growth* (World Bank, 1989); Economic Commission for Africa, *Economic Report on Africa 1990* (Addis Ababa: ECA 1990); and Institute for African Alternatives, *Alternative Development Strategies for Africa* (London: IFAA 1989).
7. M. de Larosiere, Address to the UN Economic and Social Council (ECOSOC), July 4, 1986.
8. *West Africa*, June 11, 1990, p.968.
9. See: Giovanni Andrea Cornia, Richard Jolly, and Frances Stewart, eds., *Adjustment with a Human Face...Volumes I and II* (Oxford: Clarendon Press, 1987).
10. Carol Lancaster, "Economic Restructuring in Sub-Saharan Africa," *Current History* 88, 538 (May 1989):213.
11. *Ibid.*
12. See: E. Harsch,"Recovery or Relapse?," *Africa Report* 33, 6 (1988):57.
13. Claude Ake,"The Present Crisis in Africa: Economic Crisis or a Crisis of the State?" in Julius O. Ihonvbere, ed., *The Political Economy of Crisis and Underdevelopment in Africa: Selected Works of Claude Ake* (Lagos: JAD Publishers, 1989),p.48.
14. Economic Commission for Africa, *Economic Report on Africa 1990* p. vii.
15. Adedeji, "Development and Ethics,"
16. World Bank, *Sub-Saharan Africa*, p.1.
17. This sort of propaganda can be found in the World Bank's *Accelerated Development in Sub-Saharan Africa: An Agenda for Action* (Washington, DC: World Bank, 1981).
18. Eboe Hutchful, "Structural Adjustment and Political Regimes in Africa," (mimeo), University of Toronto, 1990, p.1.
19. *Ibid.*, p. 2.
20. See: Trevor Parfitt and Stephen P. Riley, *The African Debt Crisis* (London: Routeledge,1989).
21. *Ibid.*
22. *Ibid.*
23. Eboe Hutchful, "Structural Adjustment."
24. *Ibid.*

25. See: Julius O. Ihonvbere, "Structural Adjustment, the April 1990 Coup and Democratization in Nigeria," *Africa Quarterly* 29, 3-4 (1990).
26. See: Mokwugo Okoye, "A Time of Sadness," *The African Guardian* September 24, 1990, and "Five Years of Strangulation" *Newbreed* (Lagos), 1 October, 1990.
27. See: *African Charter for Popular Participation in Development* (Addis Ababa: ECA, 1990); *African Alternative Framework to Structural Adjustment Programmes* (Addis Ababa: ECA, 1989); and World Bank, *Sub-Saharan Africa.*
28. World Bank, *Sub-Saharan Africa*, p. xi.
29. *Ibid.,* p.1.
30. *Ibid.,* p. 21
31. *African Charter for Popular Participation in Development*, p.26 (emphasis added). One significant difference between World Bank and ECA is the latter's emphasis on *transformation* as against *adjustment.*
32. Robert S. Browne, "The Continuing Debate on African Development," *TransAfrica Forum* 7, 2 (Summer 1990):35.
33. *Africa Demos* (Carter Center at Emory University, Atlanta) 1, 2 (January 1991):1.

Profile of Contributors

Adeline Apena is a professor at Russell Sage College, New York. She worked for several years at the University of Benin, Nigeria her country of origin. Dr. Apena completed her post-graduate work at the London School of Economics and the University of Ibadan. She has worked at the University of Guyana and the University of the West Indies, Mona Campus Jamaica.

Lynne Brydon lectures in social anthropology at the University of Liverpool. She has published several books amongst which is *Women in the Third World: Gender Issues in Rural and Urban Areas,* Rutgers, New Brunswick, 1989.

Ursula Funk is an anthropologist and Country Development Officer for Mozambique, Swiss Development Corporation, Switzerland.

Rosemary Galli is Senior Policy Advisor, Social Dimensions of Adjustment Project, Mozambique. She has lectured at the University of Calabar, Nigeria, University of the Azores, and Bennington College, United States.

Ralph Henry is the Head of the Department of Economics, University of the West Indies, Trinidad. He has served in an advisory capacity to several Regional Agencies in the Caribbean.

Julius Ihonvbere is a specialist in African Politics at the University of Texas at Austin. Professor Ihonvbere has published extensively and has served as a Visiting Professor at the University of Toronto where he completed his doctorate several years ago. He served as the Chair of the Department of Political Science, University of Port Harcourt, Nigeria, 1987-89.

Folasode Iyun lectures at the University of Ibadan, Nigeria. She is an active member of Development Alternatives with Women for a New Era (DAWN), and has been consulted by various institutions on health issues.

Karen Legge has done research on the Ashanti region of Ghana. She holds a doctoral thesis from the Centre of African Studies, Liverpool University, U.K.

Mosebjane Malatsi was a Visiting Fellow at St. Antony's College, Oxford University in the 1990/91 session. Before this he served as a Consultant to several U.N. Agencies including the UNDP. He is Senior Policy Analyst at Development Bank of South Africa in Johannesburg.

Adebayo Olukoshi is a Senior Fellow at the Nigerian Institute for International Affairs. He pursued his undergraduate degree at the Ahmadu Bello University where he attained first class honors in political science, and did his doctorate at Leeds University. Dr. Olukoshi served as a visiting Fellow at Oxford University in the 1989/90 session.

Hussainatu Olukoshi completed her doctorate at the University of Hull after pursuing her undergraduate work at Ahmadu Bello University, Zaria, Nigeria. She is a sociologist.

Gloria Thomas-Emeagwali teaches at Connecticut State University, New Britain. She has lectured at several universities among them the University of Ilorin, Ahmadu Bello University, and the Nigeria Defense Academy, Nigeria. She served as a Senior Associate Member and Visiting Fellow of Oxford University in the 1990/91 session and a year earlier as a Visiting Scholar at the University of the West Indies, St. Augustine, Trinidad. Amongst her edited and authored books are: *The Historical Development of Science and Technology in Nigeria* (Edwin Mellen Press, New York: 1992), *Science and Technology in African History With Case*

Studies from Nigeria, Sierra Leone, *Zimbabwe, and Zambia* (Edwin Mellen Press, New York: 1992), *Systems of Science, Technology, and Art: The Nigerian Experience* (Karnak House, UK: 1993), and *Multi-dimensional Perspectives on Africa and African Studies* (IAAS, Maryland: in press). Dr. Emeagwali is the Coordinator of African Studies at CCSU.

Gwendoline Williams is the Head of Department Management Studies, University of the West Indies, Trinidad. In the 1990/91 session she served as an honorary Visiting Fellow at Warwick University, U.K. Dr. Williams is a member of the Women and Development Study Group, Trinidad and has served in various consultancy positions.

A. Zack-Williams is a Reader at the Central Lancaster University, Preston, U.K. He has lectured at the University of Jos, as well as Bayero University, Nigeria. He was one of the founding members of the Organization of Women in Nigeria (WIN), Nigeria and has participated in several development oriented projects. He is a Member of the Editorial Collective of Review of African Political Economy (ROAPE), United Kingdom.

INDEX

Abuja Declaration, 149
Accra, 66-67, 74, 85
Adaptive Research Planning Team, 131
Addison, T., 10
Africa: Development Foundation, 36; Economic Recovery, 40, 63, 69, 80, 105-107, 110-111, 115-116, 118-119, 121, 134, 137, 147; Rice-Farming System, 61; Studies Association, 151
Afro-Caribbean, 99-100
Afro-Trinidadian, 98
Afshar, H., 11
Agribusiness, 11-12
Agriculture; Development Bank, 72, 152, 156; Extension Service, 68, 71, 77; Sector, 3-4, 6-7, 14, 20-21, 29-32, 34, 40-41, 43, 54-56, 60, 65, 69, 72, 74, 80, 83, 88, 90-96, 98, 101, 111, 114
Agro-Based Technology, 12
Ahafo, Brong, 85
AIDS, 27
Akindele, M. O., 36
Alakpeti, Logba, 66
Amansie West District, 69, 74-75, 77, 80
Amedsofe-Avatime, 83
Amedzofe, No, 78
Amerindians, 107
Andrae, G., 51
Anglican, 112
Animal, 97, 130
Antiqua, 103
Antoakrom Antoakrom, 63-64, 69-75, 77-81, 83-85
Antrobus, P., 11, 119
Appleton, 2-4, 10
Appleton, S., 2, 10
ARPT, 131
Ashanti Region, 82, 156
Association of Caribbean Economists, 11
At-risk Adolescent, 103

Atlanta, 153
Atlantic Textiles Manufacturing, 49-50
Atteinte, 30
Auty, R., 103
Awgu-Jones, A., 12
Azores, 155

Babangida, General Ibrahim, 40-41, 145-146
Bafata, 24
Bagble, 74-75, 77, 79-81, 85
Bangura, Y., 11, 51
Bank of Guyana, 119
Barbados, 11
Barrow, Dunstan, 108
Bayero University, 157
Beckman, Bjorn, 51
Bejáa, 26
Bekwai, 70-71
Berbice, 112
Berg, 11
Berlin Wall, 146
Berstein, H., 11
Bhojsons Industries Ltd, 48
Bing, Adotey, 151
BISE, 30
Bowen, N., 61
Brassa, 25-26
Brassa, Balanta, 25
Brazil, 11, 106
British Empire, 112
Browne, Robert S., 153
Brydon, L., 83-84
Brydon, Lynne, 63, 82-83, 155
Budget, 4, 39, 54-55, 59-60, 152
Budgetary, 32-33, 130
Buhari, 40
Bukh, Jette, 66
Business Development Support

Cabellero, L., 29
Cameroon, 8
Campbell, Bonnie, 10
Canada, 33, 103

Canadian Government, 85
Cape Verde, 27
Caribbean Development Women, 92
Caribbean Islands, 106
Carter Center, 153
Case of Textiles, 51
CASWIG, 112, 115-117, 120
Catholic Standard, 119
CCSU, 157
CDR, 81, 84
Central Bank of Nigeria, 36, 51
Central Statistical Office, 97
Centre of African Studies, 156
CFA, 54
Chad, 8
Chant, S., 83
Chapman, Murray, 83
Chileya, K., 128, 131
Chirwa, M., 131
Claude, Ake,, 137, 152
Cocoa Services Division, 77
Collier, Paul, 10-11, 132
Conference of Caribbean Countries,
    119
Contemproary Trinidad, 103
Context of Economic Crisis, 6, 11
Contrasting Perspectives, 1
Coordinator of African Studies, 157
Copperbelt, 124, 126, 130
Cornia, G., 10
Cornia, Giovanni Andrea, 152
Corral, Thais, 11
Country Development Officer, 155

Dakar, 23, 30
Dalmalal Limited, 43, 48-50
Datsun, 67
DAWN, 67, 156
Day Care Centers, 114
Debt Crisis, 8, 32, 51, 119, 152
Debt-Equity Conversion, 51
Decade of Women, 87
Delgado, 30
Demersy, L., 10
Democratization, 138, 147-150, 153
Department of Economics, 155
Department of Political Science, 155
Dependence, 8, 31, 41, 90, 127, 131,
    151
Deregulation, 2, 40, 55, 143
Development Bank of South Africa,
    156
Development Studies Project, 92

Development Study Group, 157
District of Jawalla, 114
Draft Medium Term Program, 103
Dressmaking, 114
During, 16-17, 20-21, 25-26, 35, 54,
    66-68, 82, 88, 93-94, 111, 114,
    138
Dutch Disease, 90-91

Earthscan, 11
Eastern Europe, 9, 141, 146
Eastern Lundazi, 125
Eastern Petauke, 125
Eastern Provinces, 124, 129
Eboe Hutchful, 10, 139, 152
ECA, 138-139, 147, 152-153
Economic; Power, 4, 18-19, 28, 30,
    39, 41-42, 51, 59-60, 117, 128-
    130, 133, 135, 139, 141-145, 147-
    148; Change, 11, 17, 61, 63, 79,
    82, 119, 122, 134, 136, 146;
    Commission, 138, 152;
    Management, 4, 8, 36-37, 43, 46,
    51, 59, 88-89, 94, 98, 102, 113,
    149, 157; Planning, 9, 27, 36, 61,
    87, 89-90, 102-103, 131, 152;
    Power, 4, 18-19, 28, 30, 39, 41-42,
    51, 59-60, 117, 128-130, 133, 135,
    139, 141-145, 147-148; Progress,
    96, 138, 145-146, 152; Recovery
    Plan, 64; Report, 10, 19, 29-30, 36,
    51, 57, 89, 103, 119-120, 136, 138,
    147, 152; Restructuring, 31, 109,
    134-136, 140, 146-146, 151-152;
    Stabilization, 2, 5, 14, 27, 51, 53,
    69, 88, 94, 100, 102, 112, 142;
    Studies, 11-12, 20-21, 63, 83, 85,
    89, 92, 118-119, 151, 156-157
ECOSOC, 152
Education, 4, 6, 20, 36, 57, 64-65,
    73-74, 76-77, 82, 84, 89, 94-96,
    102-103, 106, 109-110, 113, 117-
    118, 126, 131, 143
Egypt, 27, 41
El Salvador, 27
Elson, Dianne, 10, 61
Embroidery Group, 117
Emergency Powers, 51
Emory University, 153
Employment, 15, 17, 20, 42, 44, 46,
    65, 70, 73, 89-91, 93-94, 96, 98-
    100, 130, 148
ENDA, 30

Engendering Adjustment, 10, 87
English-speaking Caribbean, 107
EPICA, 119
Equally, 18, 25, 43, 46-47, 102, 136, 144-145
Equity, 9, 83, 85, 88, 96, 100-102
Equity Issues, 83, 85
Erionosho, O. A., 36
Ernest Wilson, 10
ERP, 64, 71, 80-81, 85, 105
Estudos, 30
Europe, 9, 33, 135, 141, 146
European Union, 29
Exploitation Within African Social Formations, 61
Exports, 11, 16, 18, 27, 32, 41, 54-55, 78, 151

Fablon Industries Limited, 43, 45, 49-50
Faculty of Education, 103
Family Life Education, 102
Family Structure, 82-83
FASCOM, 69
First World War, 64
Fishwomen, 61
Five Star Industries Limited, 49-50
Five Star Industries Ltd, 48
Five Years of Strangulation, 153
Folasade, Iyun, 31, 36
Following, 9, 14, 19, 32, 42, 55, 67, 74, 88, 90, 96, 106, 118, 127, 131
Fonseca, F. J., 30
Food Production Information, 127
Food, 2, 4, 9, 11-12, 15-16, 19-20, 25-26, 28-29, 35, 40, 57, 59, 70-72, 78, 90, 103, 109-110, 115, 123-127, 129-131, 143
Food Crisis, 12
Ford Foundation, 36
Francis, J. A., 103
Freetown, 60-61
Freetown City Council, 60
Funk, Ursula, 13, 30, 155
Future Scenarios, 10
Future The, 73, 101, 106, 112, 135-136, 139, 141, 146, 149, 151

Galli, Rosemary, 13, 29–30, 155
GDF, 116
GDP, 54, 88, 91, 93
Geba Valley, 29
Gelb, A, 103

Gender Implications, 2, 60, 119
Gender Issues, 1, 5, 11, 89, 149, 155
Gender Specific Issues, 11
Geographical Association, 127, 131
Georgetown, 109, 113, 119-120
Ghana; Government, 10, 14-21, 27-29, 31-32, 34-36, 39, 41, 47, 51, 54-56, 65-66, 68-74, 76-77, 80-83, 85, 87-88, 90-91, 94, 98, 100, 103, 108-110, 117-118, 122-123, 131, 137, 139, 144-145, 148-149; Future of, 57, 112, 135-136, 139, 147, 153; Living Standards Survey, 83; Women, 1-14, 16, 18, 20-30, 32, 34-36, 40, 42-50, 53-54, 56-61, 63-76, 78-84, 87-103, 105-124, 126, 128-132, 134, 136, 138, 140, 142, 144, 146, 148-150, 152, 155-157
Girvan, N., 11
Global Governance, 152
GNP, 18
Gold Coast, 64
Gordon, 30
Gould, J., 127, 131
Government; Printer, 51; Printery, 103; Revenue, 18, 90
Groundnuts, 14-16, 21-24, 26-27, 129
Guine-Bissau; Adjustment Facility, 30, 55; Price, 2-4, 6, 8, 10, 12, 14, 16, 18-22, 24, 26, 28, 30, 32, 34, 36, 40, 42, 44, 46, 48, 50, 54, 56, 58-60, 64, 66-68, 70, 72, 74, 78, 80, 82, 84, 88, 90, 92, 94, 96, 98, 100, 102, 106, 108, 110, 112, 114, 116, 118, 120, 122, 124, 126, 128, 130, 132, 134, 136, 138, 140, 142, 144, 146, 148, 150, 152, 156
Gunilla Andrae, 51
Gunn, Lewis A., 103
Guyana Defense Force, 116
Guyanese Women, 105, 107, 109, 111, 113, 115, 117-119
Gwendolyn Mikell, 83, 85

Haffer Industries Company Limited, 44-45, 49-50
Haiti, 108
Handem, 19, 24, 30
Handem, Diana L., 30
Hausa, 6
Health Care; Delivery System, 36;

Services, 2-4, 7, 23, 31, 33, 36-37, 55-56, 58-59, 70-71, 77-79, 88, 92-94, 106, 108-110, 113-116, 118, 122, 127, 129-130, 143
Hermele, K., 30
Hindu, 107
Hochet, A. M., 30
Hogwood, Brian W., 103
Hohoe, 66
Holy Innocents Wowetto, 114
Human Development Index, 135
Human Development Report, 136

IAAS, 157
Ibadan Nigeria, 12, 156
IFAA, 61, 152
Ihonvbere, 6-7, 133, 152-153, 155
India, 98, 103
Indo-Guyanese, 107, 119
Industries Limited, 43-45, 47, 49-50
Infant Mortality Rate Luapula, 126
Infrastructure Relief Project, 27
Institute of Economics, 132
Instituto Nacional, 30
Instrument of Structural Adjustment, 51
International Institute of Tropical Agriculture, 34
International Labor Organization, 100
International Planned Parenthood Assoc, 103
Internationalisation of Factory Production, 61
Islam, 10-11, 58

Jack, N., 103
Jackson, J., 119
Janet Bujra, 11
Jay Bee Limited, 45, 48
Jobs, Henry R. M., 92
Johannesburg, 156
Jolly, Richard, 152
Jones, J., 30
Julius, O, 133, 152-153

Kaduna Textiles Limited Workers, 51
Kanjadja Merchandise, 23
Karnak House, 157
Karuwai, 6
Kawambwa, 127
Kelvingate International, 29
Kenya, 87, 151
Ki-Zerbo, 24

Kingston, 11
Kingsway, 66
Kumasi, 70
Kwacha, 122

Lancaster, Carol, 136, 152
Lars Rudebeck, 18, 30
Lasisi, R. O., 12
Latin America, 108
Legge, K., 84
Legge, Karen, 63, 83, 156
Lewis, Theodore, 103
Loxley, John, 10
Luangwa Rivers, 124
Luapula; Mwense, 125, 127; Provinces, 124, 128-131; Zambezi, 124-125

Mabro, J., 10
Madagascar, 8
Majoub, M., 11
Malnutrition, 7, 27, 35, 56, 58, 99, 103, 123-126, 130-131
Mamdani, M., 11
Mandela, Nelson, 146
Mango, 19
Mansa, 127
Manso Nkwanta, 69-70
Mbilinyi, M., 11-12
McCullagh, R., 61
McIntosh, C. E., 103
Middle East, 33, 135, 141
Migration Process, 83
Mikell, 83, 85
Mining, 54-55, 92-93
Ministry of Agriculture, 124, 127
Ministry of Finance, 103
Ministry of Finances, 17
Ministry of Health, 124-125, 131
Minutiflora, Dioscorea, 59
Mitigate, 8, 68, 80, 108
Movement, 68, 81-82, 99, 114
Movements, 11
Mozambique, 8, 155
Mulheres, 30
Multi-dimensional Perspectives, 157
Multimedia Production Centre, 103
Muntemba, Dorothy, 12
Muslims, 107

Naira, 33, 40-42
Nairobi, 87
Nana Konadu Agyeman Rawlings, 82

National Guard, 116
National Nutrition Surveillance Program, 125, 131
National Training Board, 96, 103
National Union of Democratic Women, 23
National Union of Textile, 41
Nchelenge, 125, 127
NDK, 22
New Economic Recovery Program, 121
Newspaper, 35
NGOs, 148, 150
NIC, 64
Niger State, 34, 37
Nigeria; Defense Academy, 156; Today, 33, 61, 77, 141; Economic Crisis, 2, 6, 11, 13, 21, 23, 25, 39, 45, 47, 51, 61, 117, 133, 135, 137, 139, 141, 143, 145, 147, 149, 151-153; Institute, 11-12, 34, 103, 132, 152, 156; Journal of Paediatrics, 37; Synthetic Fabric Limited, 50; Textile Industry, 39-43, 45, 47-48, 50-51; Weaving, 46, 48-50, 66; Embroidery Lace Manufacturing Company, 43, 48-50
Nima, 85
Nimbi Project, 117-118
NNSP, 125, 131
Northern Guyana, 113
Northern Nchelenge, 125
Northern Provinces, 124, 129-130
Northern Region, 85
Northern Samfya, 125
Nwakoby, B, 37

Obadan, M., 10
Occupational Stratification, 103
Ogbomoso Community Health Care Programme, 36
Ohiorhunan, 36-37
Ohiorhunan, J., 36-37
Oil Economy, 103
Oil Windfalls, 103
Oio, 23, 25, 28
Okongwu, S. P., 51
Okoye, Mokwugo, 153
Olukoshi, Adebayo, 39, 156
Ondo State The Impact of Structural Adjustment, 33
One Year of Structural Adjustment, 51

Onimode, B, 10-11, 61
Organization of African Unity, 134
Organization of Women, 157
Orka, 144
Osinusi, K., 37
Osuntokun, B. O., 36

PAHO, 113
PAMSCAD Community Development, 81
PAMSCAD-funded, 81
Pan-American Health Organization, 113
Parfitt, Trevor, 152
Paris Club, 55
Paysanneries, 30
Pearson, R., 61
Pesquisas, 30
Petroleum, 55, 88
PHC, 32, 36
Pittin, R., 11
Political Alliances, 30
Political Impact, 11, 61
Political Regimes, 139, 152
Port of Spain, 103
Portugal, 23
Portuguese, 107
Primary Health Care, 32
Process Documentation, 36-37
Processing Company Ltd, 48
Prothero, Mansell, 83
PSIP, 88
Public Sector Investment Program, 88

Rawlings, Jerry, 144
Rayna, S. S., 30
Red Thread, 112, 117-118, 120
Regional Agencies, 155
Relatorio, 30
Rennie, Cynthia J., 103
Review of African Political Economy, 11, 29, 61, 151, 157
Rice Paddy, 14, 22
Richards, P., 61
Rienner, Lynne, 83
Riley, Stephen P., 152
Rise Hoe, 22
Rothchild, Donald, 83, 85
Routledge, 83
Rudebeck, L., 30
Rupununi, 112-114
Rural, 7, 11, 13, 20-23, 28-30, 35,

57-58, 60, 64, 66, 71, 73-74, 78,
81-85, 87, 91, 110-111, 113-115,
117-119, 122-123, 125, 127-129,
148, 155
Rural Development, 23, 28, 83, 85,
110
Rural Women, 11, 23, 28, 57, 60, 91,
111, 113, 115, 117-118
Ryan, S., 103

Saba, S., 37
SAIS African Studies Library, 83, 85
Salim A. Salim, 151
Samfya, 125, 127
SAP-related, 48
SAPs, 31, 134, 138
Saudi Arabia, 33
SDA Analysis Plans, 11
SDA Project, 8
SDA Projects, 8
SDA Social Action Program, 8
SDR, 55
Second Annual Arrangement, 29
Second World War, 66
Self-Sustaining Process of
Development, 151
Senegal, 8, 23, 27
Senior Associate Member, 156
Senior Fellow, 156
Senior Policy Advisor, 155
Senior Policy Analyst, 156
Sewing Machine Project, 114
Shaw, T., 11
Shoes, 19, 22
Shortages, 20, 26, 34, 60, 69, 108-
109
SIAS, 51
Significantly, 19, 24-26, 40, 43, 46,
76, 97, 141, 151
Social Action Project, 8
Social Cost of Adjustment, 8
Social Development Action Project, 8
Social Dimensions of Adjustment
Project, 8, 155
South Africa, 41, 146, 156
South America, 106
Southern Mambwe, 125
Soviet Union, 10, 146
Specifically, 2, 68, 71, 80, 102, 129,
136, 141, 149-150
Spinner, T. J., 119
St. Antony, 156
St. Augustine, 103, 156

St. John, 114
State Health Institutions, 37
Statement of Accounts, 36
Statistics, 11, 29, 73, 125, 132
Status Ambiguity, 82-83
Status of Women In Guyana, 112,
115, 120
Stewart, Frances, 152
Stiftung, Freidrich Ebert, 11
Study of African Economies, 11
Sunshine, C. A. Supportive Services
Susu, 80, 85
Swedish University of Agricultural
Sciences, 29
Swiss Development Corporation, 155
Switzerland, 155
Sylvia Chant, 83
Systems of Science, 157

Tailoring Workers of Nigeria, 41
TDC, 84
Technological Change Under
Economic Crisis, 61
Teenage Pregnancy, 99, 103
Tema, 83
Terms, 2-5, 7, 9, 13-14, 21-23, 27-28,
44, 54, 59, 73, 88, 107, 123-124,
126-127, 130, 136
Third World; Affairs, 7, 10-11, 88,
112, 115, 120, 156; Countries, 3-4,
27, 54, 82-83, 87, 90-91, 93, 98,
108, 119, 136-137, 140, 149-150;
Foundation, 11, 36, 61
Thomas, V., 10
Togo, 8, 64
Tombali, 21, 24, 28
Town Development Committee, 84
Transafrica Forum, 152-153
Transportation, 92, 97, 114, 119, 143
Treasury, 10, 17
Tropical Africa, 36
Tsito, 65

UCH, 34-35
UDEMU, 23
Uganda, 8
Ukwu, H., 37
Underdevelopment, 138, 141, 152
Unemployment, 41, 55, 59, 88, 91-
94, 97, 99, 102, 108-109, 135, 143
UNICEF, 27, 57-58, 61, 136
Union Papers, 120
United Kingdom, 157

United Nations; Development
    Programme, 135; Economic
    Commission, 138, 152;
    Programme of Action, 134, 137
United States, 33, 146, 155
UNPAAERD, 134, 137
Uppsala, 11, 29-30, 51
Urban Areas, 15, 20-21, 23, 25, 29,
    56, 84-85, 115, 119, 122, 128, 155
Usman, Yusufu Bala, 51
UWI, 103

Vatsa, 144
VDOs, 148
Venezuela, 106
Vierstra, G. A., 128
Volta, 64, 67, 69, 76, 79

West Indies, 92, 155-157
Western Europe, 33
Western Kaoma, 125
Western Lukulu, 125
Westview Press, 119
White, H. P., 83
Whitehead, A., 61
WID, 69

Williams, 9, 87, 157
Williams, Gwendoline, 87, 157
WIN, 141, 144, 157
Women; In Agriculture, 90-91, 96,
    103, 111, 127, 142; of Sierra
    Leone, 9, 53, 61; Studies Unit, 119
World Bank; Programs, 1-12, 29, 31,
    36, 40, 42, 55, 57, 68, 73, 80-81,
    87-90, 95, 102, 112-113, 119, 121,
    129-131, 134, 136-140, 142-145,
    147, 149-150; SDA, 8, 11, 132
World Conference, 87
World Development, 103
World Health Organization, 33

Yoruba, 85
Young, K., 61
Yusuf Bangura, 51

Zack-Williams, A., 53, 61, 157
Zaire, 134, 151
Zambezi, 124-125
Zambia Population Census, 126
Zed Press, 11
Zimbabwe, 157
Zinguinchor, 23